Reiki Rays

The Magic of Crystals in Your Reiki Journey

Rinku Patel

Copyright

© 2017, Acorn Gecko SRL

ALL RIGHTS RESERVED. This book contains material protected under International and Federal Copyright Laws and Treaties. Any unauthorized reprint or use of this material is prohibited. No part of this book may be reproduced or transmitted in any form or by any means, electronic or mechanical, including photocopying, recording, or by any information storage and retrieval system without express written permission from the publisher.

Legal Notice

Reiki or crystals are not replacements for medical assistance. Always seek professional medical support if you experience anything that requires it.

Reiki and crystals are not replacements for any professional assistance (including but not limited to relationships, finances, health etc.) Always seek the services of a competent professional if expert assistance is required.

To fully understand and to be able to apply the techniques described in this book, the reader should already be introduced to the healing magic of Reiki.

Table of Contents

7 Ways to Choose Crystals 5
Crystals Cleansing Techniques 7
Charging the Crystals 11
Crystal Programming 13
Thorough Guides to Crystals and Reiki 17
    Black Tourmaline and Reiki 19
    Amethyst and Reiki 22
    Smoky Quartz and Reiki 26
    Carnelian and Reiki 29
    Citrine and Reiki 32
    Green Aventurine and Reiki 37
    Lapis Lazuli and Reiki 42
    Tigers Eye and Reiki 46
    Red Jasper and Reiki 50
    Hematite and Reiki 57
    Turquoise and Reiki 61
    Rose Quartz and Reiki 64
Crystal Grids 69
    Infinity Abundance Grid 71
    Prosperity Feng Shui Crystal Grid 74
    The Midas Star Grid 77
    Create Harmonious Home Grid 79
    Clear Energies of Others Grid 81
    Bring New Income Grid 83
    Bring Best Partner Crystal Grid 85
    Angelic Grid to Charge Crystals 87
    Violet Flame Transmutation with Amethyst Grid 89
Crystals for Weight Loss 91
Crystals for Money 94

Crystals for Love and Relationships 97
Crystals for Healing Pets 100
The Full Body Crystal Layout 103
Crystal Water for Healing 106
Prosperity Spray..109
Psychic Attacks and Crystals...111
Diverting Psychic Attacks 114
Psychic Surgery with Crystal Wands 116
Cleansing with a Pendulum 118
Crystals and Chakras 121
Aura Sweeping with Crystals 124
Distance Healing with Crystals 126
20 Various Ways to Use Crystals...................................129
About the Author 132

7 Ways to Choose Crystals

The very first step towards working with crystals is choosing the crystals. It can be as simple and easy as you wish, or as difficult. Remember though, a crystal chooses you and comes to you, it is not the other way around.

1. The simplest and best way is to opt for the stone that attracts you, or the ones you are drawn to. That's the stone calling out to you. Don't think much about properties, you can check those later. If you can afford it, simply buy it.
2. Intuition - Just go with your gut feeling. Instead of inquiring about stone properties, just ask your intuition to guide you.
3. Another way is to touch all the stones on display and see which stone's energy resonates with yours. Personally, I do not recommend this because not everyone can feel vibrations or a stone's energy. That doesn't mean that the stone doesn't resonate with you.
4. If you are good with pendulums, check the stone's energy with a pendulum.
5. If you are buying online, just see which photo attracts or pulls you the most.

6. Buy as per properties - If you want a crystal for any particular issues, check its properties and buy. You can buy according to chakras, too.
7. Ask Reiki, angels and guides to guide you. You may start seeing certain stones frequently or you may start hearing about them. You may hear the stone name as a whisper or it may be revealed in the form of your thoughts.

If there are stones that attract you, or stones that keep coming in front of you frequently, those are the ones calling out to you. Personally, I pick crystals that choose me, the ones that want to come to me. Properties are the last thing I check in crystals. If one attracts me, if I have that pull towards it and if I can afford it, I just buy it.

Do not complicate things by thinking too much. Follow your heart and intuition and you are done.

Crystals Cleansing Techniques

Crystal healing and Reiki are two different healing modalities, and yet both go together hand in hand. When Reiki and crystals are combined for healing, the result is magnificent. Having crystals along while healing with Reiki energy is like having an extra pair of hands.

Since learning Reiki, I have developed a great liking towards crystals. I have to strictly stop myself purchasing any and every crystal I come across. Some crystals resonate with me so well, it is as if they are just meant for me. Just holding some crystals in your palms starts vibration in the Third Eye. Having bought lots of crystals, the next thing is to take care of them.

Cleansing the crystals is the most important thing to do before a healing session, setting a grid or programming for any other use. Those who are new to crystals may start wondering why crystals need cleansing. I asked my hubby to give me his crystal pendant to cleanse. He said, *"No, it's OK, it is not dirty."* Actually, crystals tend to absorb the energies around them. To diffuse the accumulated negative energy, we need to cleanse them. Cleansing removes all the previous programming too. So, once cleansed, charge and program your crystals.

Let us explore few crystal cleansing methods here

Note: *I would suggest using Reiki symbols and Reiki flow for every cleansing method.* Reiki all the cleansing materials used: salt, water, container, candle, etc.

Salt Water: Add salt to water and soak crystals for a few hours in salt water. Not all crystals resonate with salt and water, so check before soaking crystals.

Dry Salt: Place your crystals in a bowl of dry sea salt/rock salt/Himalayan salt. Make sure there are no left-over salt particles once you are done cleansing.

Running Water: Hold your crystal under a tap, stream or any form of fresh running water. Imagine all the accumulated negative energy flowing away with the running water.

Earth: Place your crystal back in its original cradle. Bury your crystals in your garden, planter or backyard. Alternatively, gather some soil in a container and bury your crystal. After removing, wipe it clean and make sure no soil particles are left.

Breathe: Hold your crystal in your palm and blow forcefully on your crystal. Imagine you are blowing a white light over the crystals. Keep blowing till you feel your crystal is shiny, or simply blow thrice with the intention to cleanse.

Flame: Just rotate your crystal 7 times over a candle flame to cleanse it. You can even pass your crystal quickly through flame.

Moon/Sun: This is one of the simplest and safest methods. Simply leave your crystals out in sunlight or moonlight. Not all crystals resonate with sunlight so please check the crystal's properties before placing in sunlight.

Smudging: Use sage or an incense stick to cleanse the crystal. Simply pass your crystal through the sage/incense stick smoke.

Reiki Only: Hold your crystal in your palm and draw Cho Ku Rei. Give Reiki with the intention to remove negative energy from the crystal.

Bell or Singing Bowl: The vibration of the bell or the singing bowl has the power to cleanse your crystals. Just play the sound of the bell/singing bowl near the crystals.

Selenite: Selenite is considered as a *'Universal Stone Cleaner'*. It does not need cleansing. Simply place your crystal over a Selenite cluster or place Selenite over your crystal. Alternatively, put all your crystals in a box and program your Selenite to cleanse all crystals in the box.

Beach: Going to a beach? Take your crystal along and cleanse with sea water.

Pendulum: Program your pendulum to cleanse the crystal and hold it over your crystal.

Third Eye: Direct white light on your crystals with your Third Eye with the set intention.

Crystal Clusters/Geode: Some crystals (Citrine, Carnelian, Selenite) don't need frequent cleansing. They can be used to cleanse other crystals, too. Simply place your crystals on the geode or cluster.

Plants: Lay your crystal beside your favourite flower or plant. Plants have the natural ability to transmute negative energy to positive energy.

Pyramid Dome: The shape of a pyramid itself is very powerful. Place your crystals under the pyramid dome. A pyramid dome neutralizes the accumulated negative energy of crystals when placed inside.

Flower Essence: Soak flower petals of any flower in water for few hours. Fill a spray bottle with this water and spray on crystals.

Again, for any of the above methods, cleansing done while invoking symbols and infusing Reiki will optimize cleansing, charging and programming.

Charging the Crystals

Between cleansing and programming crystals, there is one other step to do, and that is charging the crystals. Charging the crystals means infusing them with Divine energy. Those who know Reiki usually charge by giving Reiki to crystals. They program and charge simultaneously. But what about those who are not attuned to Reiki?

Below are a few steps to charge your crystals with Divine energy

1. **Reiki** - Draw Cho Ku Rei or Dai Ko Myo or any other symbol you are guided to on your stone. State your intention to infuse the stone with Reiki energy and let the energy flow for about 5 minutes. You can also state your intention to program for a particular issue and give Reiki simultaneously.
2. **Prayers** - You can charge your crystals with any prayer of any God or Angel you resonate with. Hold the crystal in your palms and state: *I dedicate this crystal to the energies of _____ (God or Angel name) and ask them to infuse the crystal with Divine energy.* You can say any other prayer if you wish.

3. **Mantras** - Like prayers, you can infuse your crystals with mantra energy. You can infuse with any mantra, or opt for a mantra that resonates with your wish. Hold the crystals in your palm and chant the mantra 108 times.
4. Make an angelic grid to charge your crystals with angelic energies.
5. Place outside in your yard, garden or balcony on a full moon night to infuse your crystal with Divine moon energies.
6. Rotate over a candle flame to infuse the crystal with the fire element.

Personally, I do not follow any one method. I just do as my intuition guides me. At times, I charge with Reiki, at times with prayers or with mantras. The angelic grid works best when you have multiple crystals to charge.

So, before programming your crystals, don't forget to infuse them with Divine energy.

Crystal Programming

What is crystal programming?

When you program a crystal, you are actually storing your intention and your energy in that crystal. Your crystal can be programmed for any intention and wish, just make sure that the crystal's properties resonate with your wish. When I say that you can program your crystal for any intention, I do not mean that you can program it to harm others. It will not work because, like Reiki, crystals can be used for a person's highest good only.

Why do we need to program the crystal?

Crystals have their own healing properties which work regardless of them being programmed or not. By programming, you are putting your intention into the crystal, which is then carried to the Universe, resulting in a magnificent outcome. Select a crystal that resonates with your wish. When I place my bowl of assorted tumbled stones on my altar, I intend that: *May these crystals spread their energy per their all-healing properties to heal me and my family on all levels and for our highest good. May they absorb all impure energy and transmute it to light.* If I am programming a single stone for a specific intention or for a grid, then I program the crystal for that specific intention.

Will the programmed intention stay forever?

This is quite a debatable question. According to some, crystals need programming every month or they lose their programming. Whereas some, myself included, say that once a crystal is programmed it can hold the intention for years and years, or till you de-program it.

How to program the crystal?

Before programming any crystal, make sure that the crystal is cleansed of any impure energies and de-programmed of past energies and intentions. There are multiple ways to cleanse crystals. For optimized results, we can draw Reiki symbols on crystals and charge the crystal with Reiki when programming.

Different ways to program crystals

Chanting the intention
Hold your cleansed crystal in your right palm, draw Reiki symbols over it with your Third Eye. State the intention aloud if possible, alternatively you can whisper or say it in your mind. Keep chanting your intention and stay focused, keeping all your attention and intentions on the crystal. Suppose you need love, keep chanting: *Bring Love.* Keep that thought on hold for a minimum of 68 seconds.
Repeat the process holding the crystal in your left hand.

Reiki-charged
Hold a cleansed crystal in your non-dominant hand, draw symbols and put your dominant palm over the crystal and Reiki the crystal with your intention. Again, keep the thought for 68 seconds to make the manifestation faster.

Third Eye
Take a cleansed crystal, hold it over your Third Eye, not touching the Third Eye. Beam white light from your Third Eye into the crystal. If you know Reiki, beam the power symbol and the master symbol into the crystal with your Third Eye. Think about your wish, imagine transferring your wish from your mind to the crystal. Envisage the desired outcome and place the crystal at your altar.

Tumbled stones together
If there are many crystals for general use, place all crystals together, draw symbols on them and give Reiki with the intention: *May these crystals spread their energy according to their all-healing properties to heal me and my family on all levels and for our highest good. May they absorb all impure energy and transmute it to light.*

Visualization
Hold a crystal in your palms. Think about your wish, visualize it being fulfilled. Stay focused and keep visualizing your wish and desired outcome, your reaction to it and how you would feel about it. Keep visualizing the full scenario.

Breathe intention into the crystal
Hold your crystal, enter a meditative state and stay focused on your wish. As above, visualize the desired outcome. Bring your crystal near your mouth and blow with force onto it, transferring your wish to the crystal.

Thorough Guides to Crystals and Reiki

Black Tourmaline and Reiki

Black Tourmaline is one of my very favourite crystals. I have Black Tourmaline stones, a bracelet, a pocket stone and 3 pendants. It shows my passion for this stone. I have placed stones in each room, one under my wish and pendants for my family. My kids are addicted to Black Tourmaline; they miss their pendants when I put them out during the full moon.

Every crystal lover knows that Black Tourmaline is the **MUST-HAVE** stone for its powerful healing properties. Reiki and crystals both have their own amazing healing energies and when both powerful healing energies combine, the outcome becomes doubly beneficial. The first and foremost thing to do is cleanse the crystal and infuse it with Reiki energy. We all know that crystals work with or without Reiki, but infusing crystals with Reiki results in quicker, stronger and more powerful healing.

Black Tourmaline is a stone of protection. It is also called the **Guarding Stone**. Infusing Reiki to Black Tourmaline increases its vibrations to release negativity and blockages, and gives powerful shielding and grounding.

Black Tourmaline as a Protecting Stone

- Wearing or carrying this stone shields you from psychic attacks and psychic vampires.
- Shields you from negative vibes.
- When Black Tourmaline is placed in your home or work area, it provides a protective shield around you and your home or workspace.
- Transmutes all negative energy to positive.
- Shields you from your own negative thoughts and fear.
- Stops psychic vampires sucking your energy; they won't be able to get a drop of your energy if Black Tourmaline is around your auric field.
- Wear Black Tourmaline or place it in your wallet, purse, bag, or pocket, under your pillow, add it to your bath or anywhere in your room. Place it beside electronic equipment. Make an elixir of this stone and spray on yourself or around your space. Just keep this stone close to your auric field.
- Rubbing Black Tourmaline also brings good luck and happiness.

Black Tourmaline as a Healing and Grounding Stone

- We all know how important grounding is for Reiki practitioners. Wearing or carrying Black Tourmaline makes you feel grounded and safe.
- Many times practitioners forget to ground themselves before healing a client. Always make it a habit to wear or put Black Tourmaline near the healing space to protect you and ground you.
- Black Tourmaline is directly connected to the Root chakra, hence it helps to balance the Root chakra. It also connects us to Mother Earth.
- Helps reduce stress and addiction.
- Place Black Tourmaline on your Solar Plexus chakra and give Reiki to bring clarity and power.
- Meditating with Black Tourmaline brings more light to cells.
- Stimulates balance between the left and right side of the brain.
- Also helps to balance work-and-play, pain-and-ease and high-and-low vibrations.
- Many times after giving healing, practitioners feel drained as

they have absorbed their client's energy. In that case, just hold Black Tourmaline in your palm and relax for a while. It deflects all unwanted energies absorbed from the client.

Black Tourmaline to absorb Electromagnetic Energy

• We are all exposed to electronic equipment and devices, and accumulating electromagnetic energy. Black Tourmaline helps absorb electromagnetic energy.
• Give Reiki to the stone with the intention that it absorbs all electromagnetic energy. Place the stone near equipment and devices that emit electromagnetic energy.

Black Tourmaline as a Manifesting Stone

• Write your wish on a paper. Draw symbols and chant their names.
• Fold the paper and put it under Black Tourmaline.

That's it. As simple as that. Black Tourmaline removes negativity attached to your wish and further shields it, hence quicker manifestation.

Black Tourmaline Grid

Setting a grid with Black Tourmaline removes negativity from your wishes and thus makes healing and manifestation faster.

Alternatively, you can place Reiki-charged Black Tourmaline stones in all corners of the room if you feel people with negative energy keep entering your room. This is best done at your workplace or office where many known or unknown people tend to enter. Black Tourmaline absorbs all the toxic and negative energies and provides a shield to your space.

Amethyst and Reiki

All people interested in crystals may have one stone in common and that is Amethyst. And it is also the most common stone that attracts at first sight even crystal newbies or the ones who are just buying for fashion. Have you ever wondered why Amethyst attracts people worldwide? It is because Amethyst is literally an all-purpose stone. It heals on multiple levels and it resonates with multiple issues, from protection to manifestation to spiritual development to strength and more…

It is a stone of violet flame transmutation, it brings closer connection with Archangel Michael, Archangel Zadkiel and St. Germain.

Amethyst is also considered one of the best to carry during travel, to be protected from accidents, travel-theft and robbery.

Before starting to use any stone, make sure it is cleansed, charged and programmed. Those who know Reiki can cleanse-charge-program with Reiki energy and those who don't can follow other methods you know.

Amethyst for Protection

In this age when people are competitive, jealous or knowingly or unknowingly sending psychic attacks, it becomes a necessity to protect yourself. Amethyst provides a strong shield that protects you on all levels, and it also protects from one's own negative thoughts. It also provides protection against black magic and witchcraft. Wear it, carry tumbled stones, place tumbled stones in each corner of every room, make elixirs or make grids.

Amethyst for Mental Issues

Amethyst resonates with both the Crown and Brow chakras, hence it works great to ease mental issues like stress, hyper-tension, poor focus, lack of concentration and indecisiveness. It helps students to be more focused and clear in their studies. Keep Amethyst with you and keep touching it when you are seeking clarity about something.

Keep Amethyst under your pillow if you are suffering from frequent nightmares.

It also balances emotions of being overwhelmed, over-sensitive, over-stressed, over-worked etc.

Amethyst for Crown and Brow Chakra

Those who are attuned to the Master symbol can draw Dai Ko Myo on the Third Eye, and place Amethyst over it. Placing Amethyst over the Third Eye stimulates it, giving you wider vision and clarity. Drawing Dai Ko Myo on the Third Eye helps open the Third Eye to Divine visions. Placing an Amethyst over the Crown chakra opens the Crown chakra and brings Divine wisdom.

Amethyst for Physical Issues

Amethyst is the best stone to overcome any kind of addiction, be it alcoholism, smoking, abusing or over-indulgence of any kind.

It can also ease headache and migraine. The best way to ease a headache: Place an Amethyst on the brow, above the head (on pillow) and near both ears. Relax for 20 minutes. You can give Reiki to the Crown, Third Eye and temples too.

Placing Amethyst on the navel helps with weight loss as well. It helps with hearing disorders, nervous system, digestive system, mental clutter, addiction, brain issues, cancer, eye issues, ear issues, tumours, swelling, nightmares, heart-related issues, skin issues, stomach problems and more…

Amethyst for Work / Money

Keep Amethyst with you when working on big business deals as it enhances good luck and prevents misfortune. It aids against compulsive shopping disorder or spending unwisely. It promotes saving money wisely by giving you clarity about investments.

Amethyst for Spirituality

It opens Crown chakra and Brow chakra. It brings you closer to spirituality and connects one to the Divine. Meditating with Amethyst stills mental clutter. It protects you against spiritual attacks and sends back the energy to the Universe to transmute it to light. To open your Third Eye, take a big Amethyst sphere and give Reiki to it with an intention to clear the Third Eye and open it. It is not like ball gazing, but this exercise will help stimulate the Third Eye. Gaze into it daily for 10-15 minutes. This is a must-have stone for teachers as it provides Divine wisdom and helps to share the wisdom selflessly.

Amethyst for Emotions

When using Amethyst with Rose Quartz, it provides fidelity in relationships. It heals anger, anxiety, promotes selflessness, eases emotional pain and reduces strain.

Amethyst in a Grid

Personally, Amethyst is my favourite stone to use in grids. It is an all-purpose stone, hence it can be used for multiple issues. You can either use Amethyst for the centre stone or you can use Amethyst pencils.

Combinations with other stones

Amethyst + Rose Quartz = Balance emotions

Amethyst + Sodalite = Insomnia

Amethyst + Citrine = Reduce extra expenditures

Amethyst + Citrine + Black Tourmaline = Business protection

Amethyst + Tiger's Eye = Travel protection

Amethyst + Tiger's Eye + Turquoise = Travel protection

Amethyst + Labradorite = Intuition

Amethyst + Clear Quartz = Intuition

Amethyst + Moldavite = Unbreakable protection

Start using Amethyst NOW to bring Amethyst magic into your life.

Smoky Quartz and Reiki

Smoky quartz is one of the very powerful stones, which is also called a **Stone of Power**. Smoky quartz has vast healing properties such as grounding, protection, attracting prosperity, psychic protection, EMF protection, mood changing and more... Personally, I consider Smoky Quartz a very underrated stone, it is literally an all-purpose stone which has multiple amazing healing properties.

Crystal can work with or without Reiki, but since we know Reiki I encourage everyone to Reiki your stones before you start using them. Stagnant energies get accumulated and therefore it is essential to keep our crystals cleansed and charged.

Smoky Quartz as a Grounding and Protection Stone

Smoky Quartz is associated with the Root chakra as well as the Earth Star chakra. It helps energy flow through the Root chakra to the Earth Star chakra and grounds you to Mother Earth. Carrying Smoky Quartz with you along with other protection stones can create a powerful shield against psychic attacks. It has the ability to remove any form of negativity and can also transmute it into positive energy. It also cleanses, protects and shields your aura and astral bodies by neutralising negative energies. You can place

Smoky Quartz under your Reiki bed to make your client grounded. Alternatively, they can hold Smoky Quartz before you start the healing session.

Smoky Quartz for Prosperity

The Root chakra represents basic survival which includes food, clothes and shelter; and for this we need money. If your finances are in a mess or sluggish, it indicates that your Root chakra is blocked. Smoky Quartz, being associated with the Root chakra, can enhance the manifesting of basic, personal as well as business goals. This stone is known to make wishes come true by bringing in good luck, abundance and prosperity. It also helps to manage your finances and use money effectively. Give Reiki to your Smoky Quartz with the intention to remove blockages related to money and place it in your money box or cash drawer. Carry it with you always to keep your Root chakra and Earth Star chakra active.

Smoky Quartz - Emotional Level

On an emotional level, Smoky Quartz is wonderful for people who have frequent mood swings. It removes all negative thoughts and emotions and relieves depression. It can also cut out negative emotions such as jealousy, hatred, anger, and greed, and transform them into positive emotions. It brings a certain calmness and serenity. Smoky Quartz when used with Heart chakra stones can be extremely helpful for people who are coping with grief and loss. It can eliminate suicidal tendencies. Just charge your stone with Reiki and carry it with you.

Smoky Quartz - Physical Level

Smoky Quartz on a physical level can be used to treat lower chakra issues such as the abdomen, cramps, pancreas, kidneys and reproductive system. It also helps relieve water retention in the body. It can relieve headaches, leg pain, and hip pain, just put it under your pillow or in your pocket. It also strengthens your back and spine.

Smoky Quartz - Mental Level

Smoky Quartz also enhances power, stamina, confidence and self-esteem. It gives a sense of security, as it is associated with the Root chakra. It also eliminates worries, stress, hypertension, nightmares and insomnia. Put the cleansed, charged and programmed stone under your pillow for any of these issues. Alternatively, you can wear it.

Smoky Quartz as a Meditation Stone

Using Smoky Quartz during meditation enables you to create a grounding link between the physical self and higher self. This stone is also known to stimulate Kundalini. It grounds you deeply to the earth and raises your vibrations. When you hold it during your meditation, you can easily move between an alpha and beta state.

Smoky Quartz and Feng Shui

According to Feng Shui, Smoky Quartz provides the best protection when placed near the front door. You can use a Smoky Quartz cluster or tumbled stones along with other protection stones.

Some more advantages

- It is considered the healer's favourite stone.
- Provides protection against EMF - place beside gadgets or keep near your auric field.
- When placed around 4 corners of the bed, it can help with marital communication problems.
- Zodiac sign- Capricorn.

Note - **Make sure to use cleansed, Reiki-charged and programmed crystals.**

Carnelian and Reiki

Carnelian is a stone that is orange-ish to reddish to brownish in colour, and is most famous for its bold energy. Carnelian represents boldness, motivation, warmth, joy, endurance, and courage. It emits the feeling of joy and love and also strengthens willpower. Known for its grounding and protective abilities, this stone has become one of the most loved crystals amongst crystal lovers. Fill your Carnelian with Reiki energy and see its effect amplifying. Like any other crystal, Carnelian works with or without Reiki, but combining it with Reiki optimizes the effect and makes the healing faster.

Carnelian as a Money Stone

Carnelian is also known to attract abundance, prosperity and luck. It releases undue stress and pressure in the workplace, providing determination, courage and strength. When used with Citrine or any other money stone, it amplifies the flow of abundance. It also aids bringing greater success in your career. If you have any financial or work-related wish, jot it down on paper, draw Reiki symbols and abundance symbols and place it beneath Carnelian stones.

Carnelian as a Protection / Grounding Stone

Carnelian is known to guard the house and workplace from theft, fire or any accidents. To protect your aura from bad vibrations, place Reiki-infused Carnelian near your aura. It protects from jealousy, anger, fear and self-destructive tendencies. Meditation with Carnelian helps you feel grounded and connected to Mother Gaia.

Carnelian - Physical Level

Carnelian can be used for both the Sacral chakra and Root chakra depending on its colour. It heals issues related to the Sacral chakra. Place it on your Sacral chakra and give Reiki to open and heal your chakra. Using it on the Sacral chakra can improve your sex life. It is linked with fertility and child-bearing. It helps reproductive organs and stimulates sexual energy. Women with menstrual problems should wear or carry Carnelian, and if it is charged with Reiki and intention, the healing is faster. It also helps heal impotency in men. It stimulates metabolism and helps restore motivation. It specially works with issues like fertility, sexual problems, gall-bladder, rheumatism, kidney problems, lower back problems and cell repairing.

Carnelian - Mental level

Have a look at Carnelian. Keep gazing. What do you feel? I bet most of you will feel joy and happiness. Keeping Carnelian near you soothes your overactive mind. People who have a lot of work-stress or need motivation should have this stone with them all the time. When you feel de-motivated, take a Carnelian, infuse with Reiki and hold it in your palm or keep it in a pocket to boost you up. It helps heal depression, trauma, stress, emotional wounds and sorrow from physical sources as well as the auric field. It opens creative blockages and increases creativity.

Carnelian as an Emotional / Relation Stone

It can re-ignite the lost passion between husband and wife or partners. It extradites jealousy, anger, resentment and over-possessiveness from relationships, bringing harmony and balance to them. It helps to overcome abuse of any sort and it builds self-trust within you. Also, it helps people facing a mid-life crisis. If you are angry, hold Carnelian in your palm and activate Reiki to see your anger vanish in no time.

More about Carnelian

- Helps overcome shyness.
- Energy booster and stabilizer.
- Doesn't need cleansing, also has the ability to cleanse crystals placed around it.
- Improves memory.

Note - **Charge and program your crystals with Reiki to get faster and optimized effects.**

Citrine and Reiki

Citrine is called the ***Merchant's Stone*** for its ability to attract more money as well as maintain it. The colour of Citrine varies from palest yellow to yellow to golden to honey. If you gaze at it, you will start feeling joyous and happy as it also radiates joy and happiness. It carries the energies of sun and radiates warmth and comforting energies. It is considered one of the best stones for protection. It brings money and opportunities, radiates joy and happiness and protects you and your surroundings- what else do we need?

Citrine for Physical Issues

Citrine is the stone for the Solar Plexus chakra but it resonates with the Sacral chakra and Root chakra as well. It also resonates with the Third Eye chakra and provides mental clarity, clear vision and heightened intuition. On a physical level, it supports the endocrine system and increases stamina. It increases metabolism, eventually leading to weight loss. Citrine keeps nails and hair healthy, helps rejuvenate skin, supports the pancreas, spleen and digestive system, eliminates nightmares, eliminates kidney, liver and bladder issues, helps in menstrual and menopausal problems, cures insomnia, heals hormonal imbalances, strengthens muscles, reduces diabetes, removes toxins, cures addictions and heals other issues related to the Solar Plexus chakra.

How to Use

Take cleansed Citrine and charge it with Reiki with the intention to heal any of the above issues. Lie down and place it on the Solar Plexus chakra. Leave it for 20 minutes. Do this for 21 days minimum or as required. You can also wear it or carry it with you in tumbled form. You can make Citrine water/ Citrine elixir with a specific intention and consume it.

Citrine as a Money Stone

Citrine is best known as the ***Merchant's Stone, Money Stone*** and ***Abundance Stone***. It is a stone to attract prosperity, success and all good things in life. It is the best stone to use for manifestation as it draws the things you wished for towards you, acting like an invisible magnet. Citrine has tremendous power of attraction and hence it is also used for the 7 Laws of Attraction.

Citrine is not only meant for the ones who need money, it keeps greediness and materialism at bay for already wealthy people.

Spend time with your Citrine, imagine what you desire holding your crystal and it shall manifest in reality in a better way than you ever imagined. The 7 Laws of Attraction say that if you desire anything, you have to imagine and visualize it. Citrine is used here as it has the properties to boost your visualization and imagination power.

How to Use as a Money Stone

Charge your Citrine with Reiki and:

- Wear it.

- Keep tumbled stones with you- in your purse, wallet, pocket or bag.
- Put inside your money box.
- Put inside a cash drawer.
- Put near your cash register.
- Write a wish and put under the stone.
- Place in a wealth corner of your house or office.
- Make an infinity grid.
- Use as a main stone in a crystal grid.
- Place over your cheque book or with credit/debit cards.
- A piece of Citrine kept in your purse also reduces excess money spending.
- You can make Citrine water/ elixir with intention and consume it.
- Put programmed Citrine under your pillow.

Citrine as a Family and Emotional Stone

Citrine can also solve family and team conflicts. It helps you to understand the circumstances and situation around you. Carrying a Citrine with you also attracts joy, happiness and love around you. It keeps others' jealousy and envy at bay and guards you against people who may break your heart. Family conflicts are reduced when any form of Citrine is placed in the house. It also heals heartache and depression with its joyous properties. Office politics and negativity from co-workers are eliminated.

How to Use

Charge your Citrine with Reiki to radiate joy and happiness. Wear it or place a cluster, tumbled stones or sphere in every room and office. You can make Citrine water/ Citrine elixir with intention and consume it or spray. Put programmed Citrine under your pillow.

Citrine as a Protection Stone

Citrine does not need cleansing as it does not accumulate any negative energies, although I recommend cleansing it to be on the safe side.

- Citrine not only removes physical blockages; it also removes and heals etheric and auric blockages.
- It removes blockages that hinder manifestation.
- It transmutes negativity to positivity, making your surroundings protected.
- It can keep ghosts and spirits away when set in a place where direct light comes through a window or glass. (Do not put directly in the sun.)
- People who are prone to psychic attacks or outside energies should wear or carry Citrine to protect their aura.
- It protects health, wealth, auric health, space and relationships.

How to Use for Protection

Charge your Citrine with Reiki and

- Put it in all four corners of the house or office.
- Wear it.
- Carry with you in your purse, pocket or bag.
- Make a protection grid.
- Make Citrine water/ elixir and spray on self, in house and workplace.
- Put programmed Citrine under pillow.

Other Advantages of Citrine

- Eliminates self-destructive thoughts.
- Relieves anger.
- Balances mood swings.
- Helps in concentration.
- Boosts self-confidence.
- Boosts memory.
- Enhances creativity.
- Brings mental clarity.

- Gives ability to take the right decision and action.
- Promotes success.
- Brings abundance in all aspects of life.
- Increases willpower.

I have placed Citrine in my magic money box, in a bowl full of tumbled stones, in a moon basket, in my purse and added a few beads to a bracelet.

Green Aventurine and Reiki

"We don't own crystals, we are just keepers, until they find you and you become their keeper." - **Source unknown**

Green Aventurine is considered the luckiest crystal of all, especially when it comes to prosperity, wealth, career opportunities or any other finance-related issues. Due to its 'lucky' properties, it is considered the *Stone of Opportunity*. Another beauty of this stone is that it is related to the Heart chakra, and hence resonates with anything related to the heart- be it emotional or physical. This is amongst the most sought-after stones as it relates to heart issues, wealth and opportunities. The colour of Green Aventurine may vary from light to dark green.

Green Aventurine as a Stone of Opportunity/ Money Stone

Green Aventurine actually releases stagnant patterns and blockages and creates space for new opportunities to come in. It is also known as the *Gambler's Stone* for its innate ability to attract luck and opportunities your way. It brings abundance, prosperity and attracts more financial opportunities. Carry Green Aventurine with you during interviews to improve the chances of success. Combining Green Aventurine with Citrine can grow your dead business from dooming to blooming.

How to Use

- Put in Reiki box along with the intention slip.
- Make crystal water.
- Keep in bags or pockets.
- Carry with you during interviews.
- Write your wish and put it under this stone.
- Make a crystal grid for your issue using a Green Aventurine pyramid, pencils or tumbled stones.
- Place in your cash drawer and money box.
- Wear it.
- Place near your cash counter or workplace.
- Just display at your workplace and let it radiate its energy.
- Keep at your bedside or under your pillow.

Green Aventurine for Children

Green Aventurine can improve physical growth of toddlers and teenagers. When placed near a prematurely-born baby, it can help in stimulating the baby's growth. It also boosts intelligence and memory and calms down hyper-active children.

How to Use

- Keep in bags or pockets.
- Keep under pillow.
- Wear it.
- Place at their study table.
- Make crystal water and consume.

Green Aventurine for Physical Issues

Green Aventurine is related to the Heart chakra so it can help with physical issues related to heart. It activates the Heart chakra, to keep it balanced and rotating. It removes blockages from the Heart chakra and keeps the chakra healthy. It acts extremely gently without causing any turbulence to the user. It can also help with issues like:

- Cardiac conditions.
- Helps with fertility as it is related to Cupra, the fertility Goddess.
- Blood pressure.
- Lung issues.
- Cholesterol issues.
- Skin issues.
- Allergies.
- Migraines.
- Faster recovery from surgery.
- Assists in healing any illness faster.
- Acts as an anti-inflammatory.
- Stimulates metabolism.
- Boosts immune system.
- Acts as a detoxifier and more…

How to Use

- Put in Reiki box along with the intention slip to heal the issue.
- Make crystal water.
- Place on the Heart chakra and leave for 20 minutes.
- Write your wish and put under this stone.
- Make a crystal grid for your issue using a Green Aventurine pyramid, pencils or tumbled stones.
- Keep at your bedside or under your pillow.
- Just place in the room and let it radiate its energy.
- Keep in bags or pockets.
- Wear it.

Green Aventurine for Emotions

Keeping Green Aventurine with you brings inner peace and harmony within yourself. It reduces the stress of daily life, preventing frustration and crankiness. It even calms anger, irritability and anxiety. It fights against depression and keeps you joyous, and also promotes empathy and compassion.

It also makes you emotionally stronger and helps heal emotional wounds. It is among the best stones to improve relationships that are stressed and strained. It releases unhealthy energy from relations, transmuting it to love. It helps those who are control-freaks by helping them to let go.

Green Aventurine for EMF

Green Aventurine also protects from and absorbs EMF if placed near your auric field or between you and the gadget, or near the gadget. It will also protect you from pollution if it is near your auric field. When taped to mobile phones, it protects against radiation.

Green Aventurine as Spirituality stone

Green Aventurine releases negativity, balances Yin and Yang energies, helps you to let go of attachments to old energies and promotes love, happiness and harmony. Meditating with Green Aventurine can settle negative emotions and thoughts and helps handle life-changing situations.

Green Aventurine is related to Archangel Raphael. It also honors the Goddess who is known for unconditional love- Kwan Yin. It also relates to Cupra - the fertility Goddess.

Miscellaneous Uses:

- Brings optimism.
- Enhances creativity.
- Soothes quick temper.
- Improves couples' relationships.
- Enhances homeopathic remedies when placed near medicines.
- Relieves stammers.

Combination Stones:

Green Aventurine + Rose Quartz (any pink crystal) = Harmony, Love, Joy
Green Aventurine + Citrine = Wealth, Prosperity, Luck
Green Aventurine + Moldavite = Strong partnership in relationships
Green Aventurine + Black Tourmaline = Protects against heartbreak
Green Aventurine + Moonstone = Enhanced sexuality
Green Aventurine + Carnelian = Fertility

As you can see, this is one amazing and MUST-HAVE stone. If you don't have one, go and grab one now!

Lapis Lazuli and Reiki

Lapis Lazuli is one of the most attractive and irresistible stones, even if you don't know its properties, you cannot ignore it once you have set your eyes on it. The colour of Lapis Lazuli is royal blue with gold flecks of pyrite in it. This stone is considered to be a lawyer's, writer's and inventor's best friend. Lapis Lazuli is the *Stone of Communication*.

Lapis Lazuli as a Protection Stone

As a protection stone, Lapis Lazuli can protect us from psychic attacks and psychic vampires by keeping them at bay. It keeps negative energy away from the person as well as their surroundings. It also protects us from our own negative thoughts by providing clear thinking.

Lapis Lazuli for the Throat Chakra

Lapis Lazuli resonates with the Throat chakra with its vibrant blue colour. It opens the Throat chakra and aids in communication. Your learning process becomes faster if you keep this stone near your aura. Suppose you have to give a speech in public and you are nervous or lack the confidence to speak publicly- simply carry Lapis Lazuli with you to aid with communication and speech.

Lapis Lazuli helps the endocrine system and thyroid glands. It also helps with problems related to the ears and nose. For eye infections, take a warm Lapis Lazuli heated in warm water and rub over the eye softly. You can also use Lapis Lazuli elixir for eye bath.

Lapis Lazuli encourages and promotes truth and honesty. Program and carry Lapis Lazuli to save you from liars.

Place a cleansed and Reiki-charged Lapis Lazuli on your Throat chakra while lying down and relax for a while. You can give Reiki to your Throat chakra by hovering your palms above the crystal.

Lapis Lazuli for Emotions

Lapis Lazuli brings out suppressed emotions to the surface and helps you deal with the facts related to that emotion. It helps reduce and control anger. It also aids in presenting your point of view in front of others. It helps release frustration caused by suppressed emotions. It helps to overcome issues like trauma, abuse, rape, depression, grief or loss. Also, it promotes love and fidelity in a relationship.

You can either wear a cleansed and programmed crystal or carry it around with you, or you can place it in a bowl in any room. Always use cleansed crystals and if you know Reiki, charge the crystal with Reiki and program with a set intention.

Lapis Lazuli for the Third Eye

Lapis Lazuli can be used to stimulate the Third Eye as well as the pineal gland. It enhances psychic abilities and gives clear perspective and visions. Lapis Lazuli helps to adapt new ideas and thoughts, gives a clear picture and opens the door to visions and dreams. It heightens intuition and provides wider vision and perspective. It also brings out inner truth and inner power.

Place a cleansed crystal on your Third Eye and relax for a while. Give Reiki to your Third Eye by placing your palms over the stone.

Lapis Lazuli as a Spirituality Stone

Lapis Lazuli is one of the oldest stones that is used by healers and holy workers for healing, wisdom, enhancing psychic abilities or inner visions. It is a must-have stone for spiritual growth and improved spiritual health. It maintains a connection between physical and celestial planes that results in a strong spiritual connection.

Lapis Lazuli for Meditation

Meditation with Lapis Lazuli opens the door to unknown knowledge. It can lead to past life recall as well. Meditating with Lapis Lazuli helps you connect to your Guardian Angel and spirit guides.

Meditate with this stone to manifest your wish faster as it has strong manifesting energies. Hold Lapis Lazuli in your palm, enable the flow of Reiki and set your intention to fulfil your wish. Place the stone safely or carry it around with you.

Lapis Lazuli for Physical Issues

Lapis Lazuli helps to heal: fever, epilepsy, dementia, nightmares, weakened eye sight, fainting spells, miscarriage, thyroid imbalance, vertigo, migraines, anxiety, sinus issues, nervous system, speech problems, autism, bone problems, TB, sleep problems, DNA damage, PMS, bone marrow, blood pressure, sore throat and more….

Lapis Lazuli for Mental Issues

It relieves stress and brings mental clarity. It strengthens and boosts your thinking abilities. It can calm the restless mind and clear confusion. It also increases your concentration, and therefore it's best used amongst students. It also helps to bring confidence and overcome shyness. It helps clarify thoughts in chaotic or stressed situations.

Miscellaneous use:

- Releases stress.
- Improves intellectual level.
- Enhances memory.
- Promotes honesty.
- Associated with Sagittarians.
- Helps with career and life purpose.
- Balances male-female sides of your personality.
- Helps with automatic writing.
- Enhances creativity and more…

Note - **It is always advisable to use cleansed crystals. If you know Reiki, charge your crystals with Reiki to optimize the healing and manifesting results.**

Tigers Eye and Reiki

Tiger's Eye, a multi-purpose stone with healing properties that cover most aspects of life, brings harmony and re-establishes peace. It is considered one of the best stones for students for its ability to provide clarity, focus and fast manifestation of wishes. It brings money and helps balance the flow of money. Along with harmony, focus, clarity, bringing money and manifesting powers, another top property of Tiger's Eye is that it provides protection. The combination of golden and brown colour in Tiger's Eye is like Yin and Yang, balancing spiritual and grounding energies.

The three keywords that best describe Tiger's Eye are- Protection, Abundance, Manifestation. There are 3 colours of Tiger's Eye stone- gold, blue and red.

Tiger's Eye as a Protection Stone

Tiger's Eye is considered one of the best stones for protection. It helps against evil eyes, curses, ill wishes and psychic attacks. It also makes a person feel grounded and connected to earth and nature. Tiger's Eye is best used during travel and long journeys. It brings security and stability to the user as well as protecting them at all times.

How to Use

Select the Tiger's Eye stone in any form, be it a tumbled stone, bracelet, pendant or any other form you like. Before using it, cleanse it. Charge it with Reiki energy and program it with your wish to protect. Carry the crystals with you, wear it, put it in your bag, purse or pocket, and place it in your car if you are traveling. It is totally up to you how you want to carry this stone with you.

Tiger's Eye as a Prosperity Stone

Another awesome characteristic of Tiger's Eye is its ability to bring wealth, prosperity, good luck and success. It also helps to manifest your wishes in reality. It has the innate ability to increase the flow of money. It helps you to maintain the outgoing flow of money as well as keep away from being greedy.

How to Use

Select the Tiger's Eye stone in any form, be it a tumbled stone, bracelet, pendant or any other form you like. Before using it, cleanse it. Charge it with Reiki energy and program it with your wish for prosperity. You can wear it or keep it at your workplace. Keep this stone at your workplace or house to protect from evil eyes and ill wishes and to bring in luck, success, prosperity and wealth.

Tiger's Eye for Physical Issues

Tiger's Eye is useful to treat issues related to eyes, throat, reproductive organs and the Solar Plexus. It also strengthens the spinal column, repairs fractures, alleviates pain, removes toxins, lowers blood pressure, heals organs such as the kidneys, bladder, liver, throat and colon, mends torn tissues, heals skin disorders, etc. It also gives inner strength to those who are weak or ill all the time.

How to Use

Select the Tiger's Eye stone in any form, be it a tumbled stone, bracelet, pendant or any other form you like. Before using it, cleanse it. Charge it with Reiki energy and program it with your wish to heal the affected organ, disease and chakras.

Tiger's Eye for Mental Issues

Tiger's Eye provides mental clarity during crucial phases. It enhances concentration and helps heal anxiety. It balances mood swings and boosts self-confidence and self-esteem. It promotes honesty and helps one face and accept the truth. Also, it helps you see things clearly without illusions.

How to Use

Carry the stone when you are going for a negotiation or when you need mental clarity. You can combine it with Amazonite to enhance negotiations towards your side.

Tiger's Eye for Emotions

Tiger's Eye provides inner strength and self-confidence during low phases of your life.

How to Use

Select the Tiger's Eye stone in any form, be it a tumbled stone, bracelet, pendant or any other form you like. Before using it, cleanse it. Charge it with Reiki energy and program it to provide you with inner strength, self-confidence and clarity.

Tiger's Eye for Spirituality

Meditating with Tiger's Eye promotes determination, brings positivity, connects you to nature, increases courage and hastens manifestation. The golden colour of Tigers Eye is the vibration of Christ Consciousness. It helps you contact spiritual beings associated with Golden Rays.

The 3 Colours of Tiger's Eye

1. **Golden** - Solar Plexus and Sacral chakra
2. **Blue** - Third Eye and Throat chakra. Also called **Hawk's Eye**. Along with all the above properties, blue Tiger's Eye heals

communication issues, boosts intuition and brings good luck. Heals issues related to the Brow and Throat chakra.
3. **Red** - Root chakra. Also called **Dragon's Eye** or **Ox Eye**. Along with the above properties, red Tiger's Eye increases willpower, promotes self-care and is a very powerful grounding stone. Heals issues related to the Root chakra.

Placement

You can place your Tiger's Eye stones near your main door, big windows, in your children's room, house, office, car, etc. Love and Light!

Red Jasper and Reiki

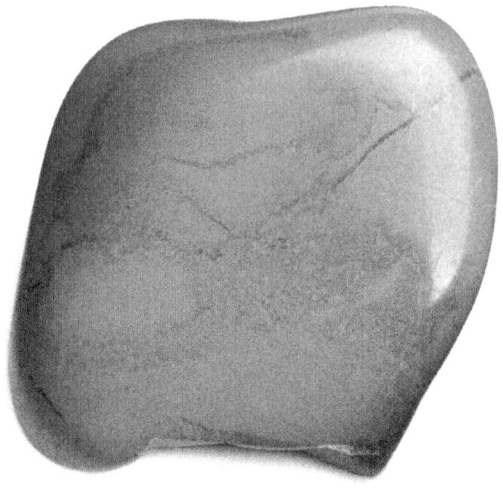

Red Jasper, a stone of grounding, protection and strength. It is associated with the Root chakra. Along with the Root chakra, it also resonates with the Sacral chakra and the Earth Star chakra. The colour of Red Jasper varies from dark orange-ish to red to reddish brown. The colour of fire and blood. Red Jasper brings stability and security in life. It is known as the **Stone of Justice** as it is beneficial in dealing with unfair situations and decreases the chances of injustice.

Red Jasper for Grounding

Red Jasper is considered one of the best grounding stones for its association with the Base chakra. It keeps you firmly grounded and rooted to Mother Earth. Whenever you feel disoriented, scattered and disorganized, carry 3 or more Red Jasper stones with you or wear it in any form.

How to Use

Cleanse the stone and empower it with Reiki energy, Reiki symbols and your intention.

- Carry Red Jasper in the form of a tumbled stone.
- Wear it in any form; I have seen amazing results when worn as an anklet.
- Put under your pillow.
- Make Red Jasper elixir.
- Sit for 10 minutes on a Red Jasper stone.
- Go for a walk with Red Jasper in your palms for better grounding.
- Massage Foot chakras with Red Jasper.

Red Jasper for Protection

As a protection stone, it not only protects the person but also eliminates negative energies, sending them back to the source. It especially protects against danger, keeping you grounded all the time. It also reverts evil magic sent towards you to its original source. Keeping Red Jasper near you shields you from evil spirits and psychic individuals. It also gives protection against negative spells. If you are traveling, you can carry, wear or put this stone in your car to prevent accidents or road robberies. Alternatively, you can hang a Red Jasper protection hanger in your car.

How to Use

Before using any stone, make sure it is cleansed. Charge your stone with Reiki energy invoking whatever symbols you are attuned to.

- Carry 3 or more Red Jasper in the form of tumbled stones.
- Wear it in any form.
- Put under your pillow.
- Make Red Jasper elixir (check Crystal Water for method). Consume or spray this water on self or surroundings.
- Keep a bowl of Red Jasper in the middle of the house or office.
- Place at every corner of your house or office.

Red Jasper for Physical Issues

If you have any nerve-related problem, take a Red Jasper and rub it softly over the nerves daily for about 15 minutes. It soothes the nerves and aids healing the problem quicker. It is extremely beneficial for people who are suffering from prolonged illness and hospitalization. It also helps to detoxify the blood and remove blockages from the liver. It strengthens muscles and eases blood circulation. It is one of the best stones to treat anaemia. Pregnant women should use Red Jasper as it makes the foetus grow safe and strong. Other physical illnesses treated include cancer, blood circulation problem, dizziness, liver problems, low blood pressure, menstruation, strength, sexual problems, stomach problems, uterus-related issues, vertigo, weakness and more…

How to Use

Before using any stone, make sure it is cleansed. Charge your stone with Reiki energy invoking whatever symbols you are attuned to.

- Carry Red Jasper in the form of a tumbled stone.
- Wear it in any form.
- Put under your pillow.
- Make Red Jasper elixir (check Crystal Water for method).
- Rub Red Jasper on affected chakra or organ.
- Put on Root chakra and give Reiki to it for optimized result.

Red Jasper for Spirituality

Red Jasper keeps your mind clear of chaos during meditation. It is also best used for astral travel and dream recalls. It is one of the best crystals for awakening and rising Kundalini that dwells at the base of the spine. This rising and awakening of Kundalini stimulates and strengthens each chakra. Meditation with Red Jasper opens up new insights and ideas related to current issues in your life.

How to Use

Before using any stone, make sure it is cleansed. Charge your stone with Reiki energy invoking whatever symbols you are attuned to.

- Hold Red Jasper in your palm during meditation.
- Keep it in front of you and keep staring at it before starting your meditation.
- Put under your pillow for dream recall.
- Carry or wear it for Kundalini rising.
- Sit on Red jasper for 10 minutes daily to raise Kundalini faster.

Red Jasper for EMF

Simply place it in the home or office near gadgets or electronic equipment to absorb EMF rays.

Red Jasper for Relationships

Red Jasper being a Root chakra stone helps with sexual problems. It promotes control and hence calms down aggressive sexual behaviour. It encourages compatibility if there is sexual incompatibility between partners. For men who have lost interest in sexual relations, this stone is for you as it increases libido.

It also helps jealous and possessive people overcome these issues. It can be beneficial to women who are having difficulty conceiving a child. For pregnant women, it protects the foetus and ensures safe childbirth.

How to Use

Before using any stone, make sure it is cleansed. Charge your stone with Reiki energy invoking whatever symbols you are attuned to.

- Both partners should wear this stone if there is a sexual problem.
- Put under the pillow of both partners.

- Both should consume Red Jasper elixir.
- Place a few stones on the bedside table.
- For jealousy and possessiveness, wear in any form or carry it with you.
- For pregnancy, wear or carry in any form.

Red Jasper for Career / Work / Money

Red Jasper brings focus and clarity to stay rooted in your work. It is helpful to keep your thoughts focused and concentrate on the work at hand. It enhances your creative level and is one of the best stone to manifest ideas. It is considered the best stones for people who are in performing arts, expressive arts and who are amidst audiences like actors, dancers, athletes, creative work teams, etc. It is also good for people who require physical strength like cops, waiters, construction workers, body-builders, wrestlers or people with a high level of activity. Being an earth element stone, it also helps attract abundance.

How to Use

Before using any stone, make sure it is cleansed. Charge your stone with Reiki energy invoking whatever symbols you are attuned to.

- Carry in the form of tumbled stones.
- Wear it in any form.
- Place in your workplace.
- If you feel weak physically or mentally, simply hold it in your palm.
- Put under your pillow.

Red Jasper for Emotional Issues

Red Jasper promotes emotional strength and courage. It is highly advisable for people suffering from or who have suffered domestic violence, violent behaviour, aggressive sex, rape, being bullied, harassment, etc, as this stone brings you extra and much-needed courage to get over it and come through it. It can help people with suicidal tendencies by providing the will to live. Also, it is good for people who have to take care of ill patients or relatives for strength.

How to Use

Before using any stone, make sure it is cleansed. Charge your stone with Reiki energy invoking whatever symbols you are attuned to.

- As above, carry tumbled stones or wear in any form.
- If it is aggressive sex, place lots of tumbled stones in the bedroom.
- For domestic violence, place in the room it takes place.
- Place in all rooms.
- Spray Red Jasper water.
- If you are upset, holding Red Jasper or chanting with a Red Jasper rosary will make you feel centred and soothe your emotions.

Red Jasper for the Root Chakra

Red Jasper is a Root chakra or Base chakra stone which helps the user feel connected and grounded to Mother Earth. Put it on your Base chakra to cleanse and remove blockages from the chakra. Carry or wear it when your Root chakra seems imbalanced. When your Root chakra is balanced, you regain your strength, stamina and willpower. It brings back your own power, stamina and willpower.

Red Jasper for Feng Shui

As per Feng Shui, Red Jasper can be placed in the centre of the home for balanced Yin and Yang energy and protection. For relationships, place it in the southwest corner of the house.

Red Jasper and Combinations

Creativity- Combine with any creativity stones like Carnelian, Amazonite, Green Aventurine, Tiger's Eye, Citrine, Moonstone
Grounding- Combine with any grounding stones like Smoky Quartz, Hematite, Howlite, Tiger's Eye, Snowflake Obsidian, Bloodstone, Black Tourmaline
Kundalini awaken/rise- Combine with Green Serpentine, Shiva Lingam, Tiger's Eye, Jet, Cinnabar, Moldavite
Pregnancy- Combine with Unakite, Carnelian, Moonstone
Protection- Combine with Black Tourmaline, Fire Agate, Hematite, Tiger's Eye, Smoky Quartz, Obsidian, Onyx

Red Jasper for Ritual

Using Red Jasper with red or burgundy candles and bright red flowers can bring manifestation faster. The essential oils that go best with this stone are ginger, mint and cedar wood.

So, if you don't have Red Jasper, go and bring one home now!

Hematite and Reiki

Hematite is one of the most irresistible stones I have acquired. Before getting into in-depth details about this stone, let me tell you about its attractiveness. The colour of Hematite is dark metallic steel grey, and it glimmers. The one word to describe Hematite is 'Elegant'. When Hematite beads are combined with other beads for a bracelet or necklace, it gives extreme elegance to the product with its metallic dark steel grey colour. It increases the beauty of other stones combined. Okay, enough talking about just its outer beauty.

In ancient times, Hematite or Haematite was known as bloodstone but not the same bloodstone that we know today. Hematite derived its name from the Greek word *Haema* which means blood. When it is powdered or in a clay form, the colour of Hematite is red. It is considered the *Stone of Blood*.

Let me Start with How to Use

First and foremost, cleanse and charge it with Reiki. If you are attuned to symbols, draw symbols and charge with Reiki. Program it with the intention or alternatively just wear it directly after charging. I prefer programming it with the intention that it acts as per all its properties, which include grounding, protection, blood purification and more… If you don't know Reiki, don't get disheartened, you can continue without Reiki too. Just put the crystal in salt water for 3-4 hours to cleanse it. Once cleansed, take it in your palm and chant a mantra or any prayer to charge it. Put your intention and hold your intention for 68 seconds. Keep stating your intention, or you can visualize the outcome of your intention. That's it.

Usage

- Carry or wear it.
- Place a bowl full of Hematite at the centre of the house.
- Grid it with Black Tourmaline by putting it in all corners of the room.
- Make a crystal grid.
- Make an elixir without putting it directly in water.
- Put under your pillow.

Hematite for Grounding

Hematite is the stone for the Root chakra as well as the Earth Star chakra and hence it is amongst the best stones for grounding and protection. Carrying Hematite keeps one centred and focused even at the most stressful times. It makes one feel safe and secure by strengthening the connection with earth.

Hematite for Protection

Hematite not only dispels negative energies but it also transmutes negative energy into positive. Some also believe that it throws back all the negative energy to the source and therefore if you are using this stone, you have to keep your thoughts positive. Personally, I feel it transmutes negative to positive. It releases all the negative energies and auto-recharge positive energy.

This is an excellent stone for those who stay outdoors, interact with new people and come across many people daily. It protects you from absorbing negative vibes, evil intentions and negative energies from others. This is a must-have stone for adventurous people as it protects against bleeding if anyone is injured.

Hematite for Physical Problems

Since Hematite is considered the 'Stone of Blood', it is one of the best stones to heal any blood-related disease. It acts as a blood cleanser and helps with blood circulation. It also prevents excessive menstrual flow and aids to regularize the menstrual cycle.

It can also be used to heal headaches, heat stroke, spine alignment, dizziness, weak legs, leg cramps, kidney issues, etc. If you suffer from sciatica, go for this stone now because it helps the user connect to the Earth Star chakra. Sciatic nerve problems happen when the person is disconnected from the earth and is out of balance.

It can also help with skin problems, as well as heal cuts and wounds.

Hematite for Mental Strength

Hematite promotes logical thinking and keeps the mind organized and calm, preventing anger, stubbornness and obsessions. It provides mental strength and keeps the user away from addictive habits. It also enhances memory and brings focus. It creates photographic memory in one's mind. It also brings mental clarity and provides determination and willpower.

Hematite for Spirituality

In ancient times, people used to burn candles in front of Hematite. The Hematite is placed in such a way that the candle flame reflects on it. Then they stare at the reflecting flame and think about the problem they need an answer for, or think about the wish to be fulfilled.

Hematite Miscellaneous Uses

1. Instead of cleansing Hematite in water, bury it under rock salt or place near any cleansing crystals

like Selenite, Carnelian or Citrine. You can also cleanse it by drawing Cho Ku Rei or Dai Ko Myo and giving Reiki to it.
2. Place it amidst other crystals to cleanse those crystals.
3. Direct elixir is not advisable as it contains iron ore. So, make an elixir by placing Hematite around the container.
4. Use it on the Solar Plexus chakra to improve and increase willpower.

Hematite and Other Stone Combinations

Relationships- Always carry Hematite + Rose Quartz, Hematite + Rhodonite with you for healthy loving relationships.
Grounding- Combine with Black Tourmaline, Red Jasper, Smoky Quartz or any other grounding stones.
Protection- Combine with Black Tourmaline, Citrine, Tiger's Eye, Snowflake Obsidian or any other protection stones.
Overcome Addiction- Combine with Amethyst, Carnelian or Red Jasper.
Stimulate Willpower- Combine with Carnelian, Citrine or Malachite.

Use it with lower chakra stones to strengthen and balance the chakras.

One Small Ritual to Perform with Hematite

Take a Hematite and hold in your palms. Sit quietly and pour all your troubles and worries into this stone. Be very clear, as if you are talking to your friend. Bury it somewhere in earth. Mother Earth will neutralize all the negativity you have poured into the stone. As simple as that!

Turquoise and Reiki

Turquoise is known as the ***Stone of Heaven*** as it builds a bridge between the wearer and the spiritual realm. The colour of turquoise varies from sky blue to peacock blue to sea green. The black/brown veins strengthen all the healing properties of this stone. It is one of the most powerful stones to work with, mainly because of its resonance with 3 chakras: the Third Eye chakra, the Throat chakra and the Heart chakra. It promotes and unblocks your hidden potential and creativity from deep within you.

Before using any stone, it is very important to cleanse and charge it. It is extremely easy, just hold in your palm and draw Cho Ku Rei and give Reiki with intention to cleanse it. After 3-5 minutes, draw another Cho Ku Rei and Sei He Ki and other symbols you want to invoke, give Reiki while chanting a prayer or mantra. The proper in-depth method of cleansing and programming is mentioned in previous chapters.

Turquoise as Protection

Turquoise is also called the ***Purification Stone*** for its ability to protect the wearer from all kinds of negative energies as well as shielding from outside pollution. It purifies the aura on all levels. It is also one of the best stones to carry while traveling. Even though it is a stone resonating with upper chakras, it will always keep you grounded and rooted to Mother Earth.

Turquoise for Healing

On healing terms, wearing Turquoise helps balance and align all your chakras. It helps people who are suffering from depression and mood swings by keeping them joyous. It is basically an all-purpose physical healing stone, as it has the ability to heal the whole body. It is best for issues like sore throat, cold, cough, headaches, migraine, eye and ear issues, blood pressure, acidity, stomach problems, viral infections, brain-related issues, nutrient absorption and more…

Turquoise for Finances and Career

As a finance stone, it helps you make wise financial decisions, helps you invest and save money wisely and stops you from being a spendthrift. It helps you to communicate clearly, leaving no space for misunderstanding. It is advisable to wear turquoise whenever you have to make financial deals. A highly recommended stone for speakers, teachers, lawyers and all who are in a career where communication needs to be crystal clear.

Turquoise for Emotions

As I said earlier, it is best for healing depression and mood swings. Wearing turquoise promotes self-love, self-worth, self-awareness and self-forgiveness. It promotes generosity and affection and opens your heart to accept love. It opens your Heart chakra and allows giving and receiving love without inhibitions. It also promotes marital bliss to the fullest.

Turquoise for Chakras

Placing a turquoise on the Third Eye chakra will help release old vows. It increases your intuition and allows the soul to be free of all bindings. As a Throat chakra stone, it aids with crystal clear communication and helps you voice your opinions. If you are shy, this stone will help you come out of your shell.

Turquoise for Manifestation

It is one of the best manifesting stones. It brings good luck to the wearer and is said to bring double luck if gifted to someone.

Combining Turquoise with Other Stones

Weight loss = Turquoise + Iolite + Apatite
Grounding = Turquoise + Hematite + Red Jasper/ Red Aventurine
Protection = Turquoise + Black Tourmaline/ Smoky Quartz
Love = Turquoise + Rose Quartz
Intuition = Turquoise + Amethyst + Clear Quartz
Manifestation = Turquoise + Lapis Lazuli
Money bringing and saving = Turquoise + Citrine
Luck = Turquoise + Green Aventurine
Confidence and Focus = Turquoise + Carnelian

Just work with Turquoise and see how the magic begins.

Rose Quartz and Reiki

Rose Quartz, the stone of love and the heart, is one of the most sought-after stones. The first word that comes to mind on seeing a Rose Quartz is 'Love'. It has quite soothing and calming energies. Being a love stone, it promotes unconditional love, self-love and fidelity. Apart from being a love stone, Rose Quartz provides harmony, calmness, peace and heals an aching heart, relations, emotions and the inner child. The colour of Rose Quartz varies from pale pink to baby pink to hot pink.

Before starting to use your stone, it is extremely important to cleanse it, charge it and program it. If you know Reiki, charge your stone with this Divine energy.

Rose Quartz for Relationships

Working with Rose Quartz is the easiest way to heal relationships, be they romantic, friendly, parent-child or any other relation. It can also be used to attract new love, a soulmate or new friends. It is one of the most used stones for rituals of love and relations.

A few pieces of Rose Quartz in a bowl kept in the living room promote harmonious relationships in the house. They bring harmony and peace to the house. Simply take a few stones and draw Reiki symbols over them (skip if you are level 1 or don't know Reiki) and infuse the stones with Reiki energy with the intention to radiate harmonious and peaceful energy. Those who don't know Reiki, take a stone in one palm and cover it with another. Intend that it radiates harmonious and peaceful energies in the house. It can also help to calm down over-active children and pets.

You can make Rose Quartz elixirs and spray in the house, on the self, family members and pets.

Rose Quartz for the Workplace

Putting Rose Quartz in the workplace (office or shop) radiates loving energy to provide harmony. It keeps the atmosphere calming and peaceful and eliminates jealousy and envy from colleagues. Combining Rose Quartz with Black Tourmaline at the workplace helps reduce gossip and politics in the office against you. (Program your crystals with your intention with or without Reiki.)

Rose Quartz for Emotions

Rose Quartz radiates joy and happiness and keeps your emotions balanced. It heals an aching heart, heals the inner child and brings unconditional love to the soul. It helps you to let go of the past and fosters forgiveness and empathy. It removes suicidal thoughts by giving confidence in oneself. It promotes self-love and self-care.

Rose Quartz for Meditation

Meditation with Rose Quartz releases guilt, anger and self-criticism, and promotes unconditional love, acceptance and compassion. It also helps to release stagnant energy from the Heart chakra.

To release accumulated stagnancy, blockages and negative emotions, lie down on your stomach and ask someone to place a pre-programmed big Rose Quartz or a few tumbled stones on the back of your Heart chakra. Leave it there for 20 minutes. Do this for 21 days.

Rose Quartz for Mental Issues

Since Rose Quartz is the stone that radiates loving, harmonious and calming energies, it helps reduce stress and anxiety.

Rose Quartz for Physical Issues

Rose Quartz is a 'Heart Stone' and hence it resonates with the Heart chakra. It can help with physical issues related to the Heart chakra. It soothes minor cuts and burns. Just rub the stone on the affected area if you can or if it is painful, hover the stone in the aura over the affected area. It also helps with fertility issues, sexual issues and reproductive system issues.

Rose Quartz for Beauty

Massage lightly on your face to make your skin smooth and babyish. Add a few pieces in your creams and lotions or place around the bottles. You can make crystal water/elixir to make your skin youthful, healthy and soft. Put a piece of Rose Quartz in an ice tray with water and use Rose Quartz ice to massage your face. Rose Quartz beauty tips can be extremely beneficial for those who run salons or beauty parlours.

Miscellaneous Tips

1. Can be used in rituals related to love, relations, harmony or fertility.
2. Related to the Heart chakra, Higher Heart chakra (Thymus chakra).
3. Brings faith and hope, and increases positive energy.

Combining Rose Quartz with other stones

Rose Quartz + Red Jasper= Love and Passion
Rose Quartz + Black Tourmaline = Spread harmony and reduce gossip and jealousy
Rose Quartz + Rhodonite = Helps relieve pain and move on
Rose Quartz + Amethyst = Release stress and tension
Rose Quartz + Moldavite = Peaceful transformation

Rose Quartz + Citrine = Harmony and love with money
Rose Quartz + Green Aventurine = Bring opportunities to attract new love
Rose Quartz + Carnelian + Unakite = Fertility

So, start working with Rose Quartz now.

Crystal Grids

Infinity Abundance Grid

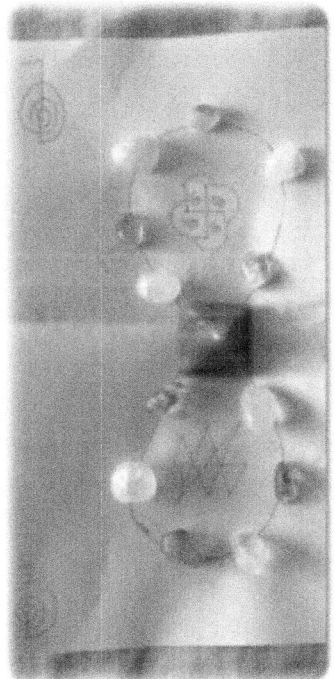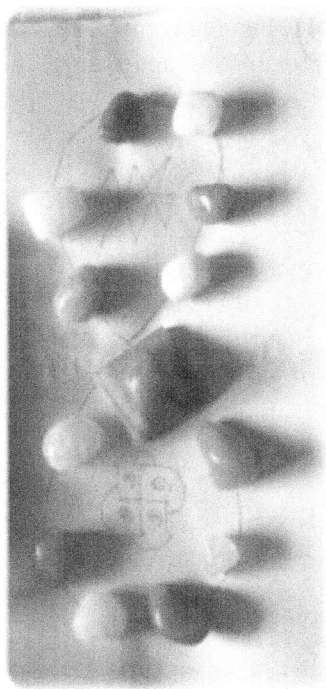

Here, abundance doesn't mean only money. Abundance means anything abundantly, whatever you desire - be it money, love, protection, peace or whatever.

Money, a single word, which help us achieve and fulfil our goals and wishes along with your hard work and luck. Money doesn't grow on trees but we can try things that attract more money into our lives. Yes, I totally and fully agree that money is not everything in life, money cannot buy love and peace. But as the saying goes, *"Better to cry in a Ferrari than under a bridge."* Again, wanting money doesn't mean you go and dupe people. Hurting anyone for monetary gain is a strict no-no. I prefer working with crystals to bring and attract more money into my life.

Love, a single word, without which survival becomes impossible. Love in any form is a necessity, not just between partners. Love for peace and humanity, love towards the elderly, love for orphans, love for animals and pets... It is a feeling that flows freely, it cannot be forced on anyone or from anyone. So, what do you do when you are in a relationship and love has vanished, that old passion is gone? You can't force anyone to love you back. Here again crystals help, to bring love, luck and that old passion back.

As I always say, crystals and Reiki when combined bring magical and amazing results. Working with a crystal grid is a sure way towards manifesting your goals and desires. There are different types of grid layouts which you can work with. Here I will show you an infinity abundance grid. By abundance, I do not mean only money. This infinity abundance grid is about Abundance of money, Abundance of love, Abundance of peace, depending on the crystals you use. This is a very simple and non-fancy grid which you can make easily.

For money, you need:

- 6 Citrine tumbled stones (or any money stones)
- 6 Clear Quartz tumbled stones
- 1 pyramid/sphere/cluster (money stone)
- 1 wand to connect and charge the crystals

For love, you need:

- 6 Rose Quartz tumbled stones
- 6 Green Aventurine tumbled stones (any love stone)
- 1 pyramid/sphere/cluster (love stone)
- 1 wand

For protection, you need:

- 6 Black Tourmaline tumbled stones
- 6 Smoky quartz (any protection stone)
- 1 pyramid/sphere/cluster (protection stone)

- 1 wand

Select crystals as per your requirement. You can use any wand to charge and connect the grid.

How to Make a Grid:

- Assemble all the cleansed crystals. Hold 1 set of crystals in your palm, draw Cho Ku Rei over it and rotate clockwise 7 times saying: ***Purify, Purify, Purify***. Place the other palm over the crystals and let Reiki flow for 5-10 minutes. This is the time when you put your intentions into the crystals. While charging crystals with Reiki, think of your intention, such as abundant money, abundant love, abundant protection or whatever. Do the same with all sets of crystals.
- Take an A4-size paper and draw a big infinity symbol. You can take a ready-made printout too. On 4 corners of the paper, draw the power symbol to seal the energy.
- Place the pyramid/sphere/cluster at the centre of the symbol where two lines of '8' intersect.
- Place Citrine and Clear Quartz or Rose Quartz and Green Aventurine or Black Tourmaline and Smoky Quartz tumbled stones alternatively as shown in the illustration.
- Take a wand, rotate over the pyramid thrice saying: ***Connect, Connect, Connect***.
- Now, starting from the top middle stone, rotate wand clockwise thrice over each stone saying: ***Connect, Connect, Connect***. (You can start with any stone, not necessarily the topmost)
- Once you complete the full infinity 'connect' cycle, bring the wand back to pyramid, rotate thrice and say ***Activate Activate Activate***.
- Now make a Reiki-infused Chi Ball and place it over the grid with the intention to keep it charged for the next 7 days. Place a Chi Ball every week. In between, if needed, cleanse your crystals and reset your grid.

Prosperity Feng Shui Crystal Grid

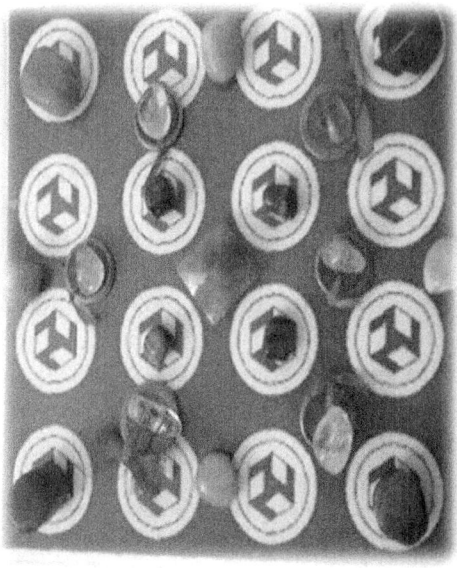

Using Feng Shui brings a positive flow of energy into one's life and surroundings, bringing prosperity, luck, love, protection and good health. Here we merge Feng Shui with crystals which will amplify the energy to another level.

This is one of the simplest grids and easy to make.

Feng Shui Prosperity Grid

- Grid base - Antahkarana base multiple squares
- Green Aventurine tumbled stones - 4
- Jade tumbled stones - 4
- Citrine tumbled stones - 6
- Tiger's Eye tumbled stones - 4
- Chinese coins - 6
- Green Aventurine/ Citrine/ Tigers Eye/ Amethyst/ Clear Quartz pyramid

Your crystals should be cleansed, programmed and charged with Reiki or any mantra.

1. Your Chinese coins have 2 symbols on one side and 4 on the other side. You have to place the coins with 4 symbols facing up.
2. Start by placing your pyramid at the centre of the Base.
3. Next, on 4 surrounding squares, place 4 Tiger's Eye.
4. Place 6 Chinese coins with 4 symbols facing up around the Tiger's Eye, as shown in the picture. Place Citrine over each Chinese coin.
5. Place Green Aventurine on 4 sides- top, bottom and both sides; refer to picture.
6. Place 4 Jades on the 4 corners.
7. Once the setting is done, take a wand and rotate clockwise over the pyramid thrice and say: **Connect, Connect, Connect**. Again, rotate thrice and say: **Activate, Activate, Activate**.
8. Make a Chi Ball and set an intention to attract abundant prosperity to you. Release it over the grid.

No need to add any intention slip.

Infinity Feng Shui Prosperity Grid

- Infinity symbol base
- Green Aventurine pyramid
- 8 Tiger's Eye
- 6 Chinese coins
- 6 Citrine

This grid will help bring a constant flow of money infinitely.

1. Starting from mid pyramid stone, place your crystals and Chinese coins as shown in the picture.
2. Once the setting is done, take your wand and trace a line over the stones in the air; connect them. Starting from the pyramid, trace the whole infinity symbol thrice.
3. Rotate clockwise over pyramid thrice and say: **Connect, Connect, Connect**. Again rotate thrice and say: **Activate, Activate, Activate**.
4. Make a Chi Ball and set an intention for infinite cash flow and release it over the grid.

You can cleanse and reset the grid once a month.

The Midas Star Grid

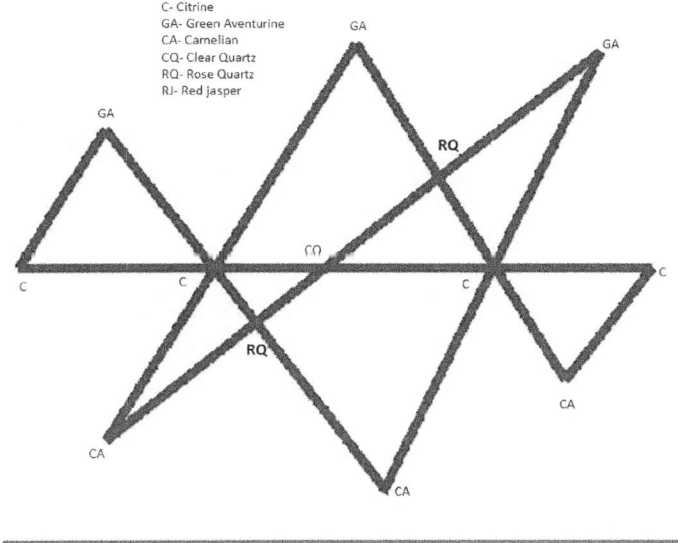

RED LINE- RJ or GARNET

The Midas Star is known as a prosperity symbol but 'prosperity' doesn't only mean money. Prosperity can bring about success in inter-personal relations, luck and harmony along with money. So here we will be using the Midas Star symbol with crystals to manifest prosperity in all aspects of our life.

The red line under the Midas Star helps grounding energies.

Required

Citrine- 4
Green Aventurine- 3
Carnelian- 3
Rose Quartz- 2
Clear Quartz Cluster- 1
Red Jasper/Garnet- Depending on the size of the red line and the size of your stones.
Approximately 6-8 stones.

1. First, cleanse, charge and program your crystals for prosperity in money, relations, luck and success. If you know Reiki, charge and program your stones with Reiki with an intention to bring success in luck, relations and money.
2. You have to place the stones as shown in the grid diagram.
3. Citrine- Money- As you place each Citrine, say thrice: *Bring in financial abundance now and forever.*
5. Green Aventurine- Luck- As you place each Green Aventurine, say thrice: *Good luck in money, relations, health and success follows me everywhere now and forever.*
6. Carnelian- Success- As you place each Carnelian, say thrice: *Success is part of my being in all aspects of my life.*
7. Rose Quartz- Harmony- As you place each Rose Quartz, say thrice: *My house, surroundings and all my relations radiate harmonious energies.*
8. Clear Quartz- Magnify- As you place Clear Quartz, say thrice: *Amplify the energies of all the stones.*
9. Red Jasper/ Garnet- Grounding- As you put each stone, say thrice: *I am totally grounded and protected.*
10. With your wand, trace the Midas Star, connecting all the crystals. Rotate clockwise over the grid and say: **Activate, Activate, Activate.**

Leave the grid for a minimum of 21 days.

Enjoy the abundance of your life!

Create Harmonious Home Grid

We live a life that's way too fast, with not enough time, less patience, less compromise and more stress. This leads to strained relationships, disputes, arguments and fights, which affect the energy of the house. In some cases, there are strained relations between family members, which again disharmonize the home environment.

Here we merge Reiki and crystals which in return will create harmony in the house by regenerating and rebalancing the energies.

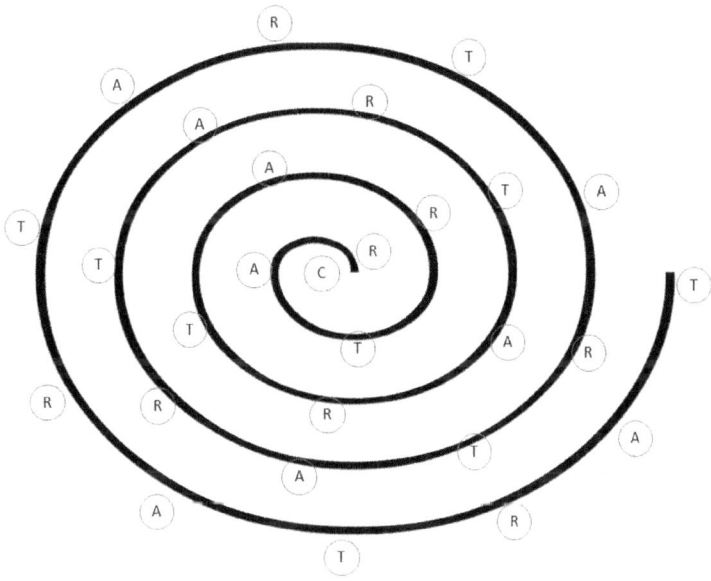

Required

Tiger's Eye- 9
Rose Quartz- 9
Amazonite- 9

Clear Quartz Cluster/ Rock/ Pyramid/ Sphere- 1 Wand

You can place more tumbled stones if you wish instead of 9 each

1. First, cleanse, charge and program your crystals. If you know Reiki, charge and program your stones with Reiki with an intention to harmonize the house energies.
2. Draw a spiral on some paper. With your finger trace Dai Ko Myo over the spiral. If you are not attuned to Dai Ko Myo, trace Cho Ku Rei over the spiral. And if you don't know Reiki, just skip this step.
3. Start placing your crystals from the outer end at regular intervals. Tiger's Eye- Amazonite- Rose Quartz.
4. While placing each Tiger's Eye, say thrice: *Bring in grounding, stable and protective energies.*
5. While placing each Amazonite, say thrice: *Radiate family joy, happiness and harmony.*
6. While placing each Rose Quartz, say thrice*: Radiate unconditional love.*
7. Place Clear Quartz at the inner end and say thrice: *Amplify the energies of all the other stones in the grid.*
8. With your wand, trace a spiral over the crystals, connecting all of them. While connecting, say thrice: *I create harmonious, joyous and loving energies in my home.*
9. Make a Chi Ball, add Reiki symbols if you are attuned. Pray to Archangel Chamuel: *Dear Archangel Chamuel, please fill my house with Divine love, joy and happiness. Thank You.* Pray to Archangel Raguel: *Dear Archangel Raguel, please resolve all kinds of conflicts, sadness and heartache from everyone staying in this house and fill the house with love and light.*

Release the Chi Ball on the grid. Leave the grid as it is for a month and then cleanse the stones and remake it.

Harmonize your home atmosphere now and stay happy!

Clear Energies of Others Grid

The energy residues of others get accumulated in our house and working space whenever they visit. Some people send psychic attacks knowingly or unknowingly to your home, family life, workplace or business. Your workplace or house may get affected by the evil eye even if the person has never visited your house/workplace. This grid will help draw out all the negative energies, evil eyes and psychic attacks and transfer them to Mother Earth. We will be using a pentagram shape here as a grid base, as the pentagram is known for providing strong protection.

Required

Black Tourmaline (BT)-3
Smoky Quartz (SQ)- 2
Citrine cluster or 5-6 tumbled stones
Wand
Himalayan/Rock salt
Pentagram drawn on A4 paper (optional)

1. First, cleanse, charge and program your crystals for protection. If you know Reiki, charge and program your stones with Reiki with an intention to remove all negative and lower energies.
2. Draw a pentagram on paper. You can also draw a pentagram with Himalayan/Rock salt directly on a surface where you want to create the grid. If you are using paper, draw with salt on paper.
3. Now on the left most, right most and top point of the star, place Black Tourmaline and say thrice: *Remove negative energy from this house/office/shop and transmute it to light.* For each stone, you must say thrice while placing.
4. On the other 2 points of the star, place Smoky Quartz and say thrice: *Ground all unwanted energies from this house/shop/workplace.*
5. Place Citrine cluster or all tumbled stones in the middle of the star and say thrice: *Bring in Divine light and joyous energies to this house/workplace/shop.*
6. With your wand, trace the star connecting Black Tourmalines and Smoky Quartzes. Say thrice: *I bring in Divine protection and Divine light to this house/office/shop now and always."*
7. Make Chi Ball and call upon Archangel Michael and pray: *Dear Archangel Michael, please cut all the unwanted negative cords from this house, remove all kinds of negative and lower energies and create a purple shield around my house and outer areas. Thank you.* If you know Reiki, add Cho Ku Rei, intone its name thrice and say: **Protect, Protect, Protect**. Release the Chi Ball on the grid.
8. Stare at the pentagram and visualize it in purple or gold light shining brighter and brighter.

Don't touch the grid. You can add the names of your family members by writing on chits and placing beneath the Citrine. You can cleanse your grid once a month or when you feel it has accumulated lots of negative energies. Re-make after cleansing.

Bring New Income Grid

At times, it so happens that one is constantly in need of extra cash, regular income is not enough and you are always looking for new mode of earning extra income. This grid will help draw new income to your business/ house. The extra income can be in the form of a new job, new business, bonus, new orders, etc.

Here we use a house-shaped grid with an intent to bring more money to the house/ business.

Required

Cinnamon powder, to draw the house
Citrine (C)- 2
Green Aventurine (G)- 2
Smoky Quartz (S)- 2
Any 1 stone of your choice
Wand

1. First, cleanse, charge and program your crystals to bring in new income. If you know Reiki, charge and program your stones with Reiki with an intention to bring more income to your house/ business.
2. On a paper or any flat surface, draw a house shape with cinnamon powder. Cinnamon is known to attract more money and hence we are using cinnamon powder here.
3. Inside the triangle write Switchwords for money: **Divine-Find-Count**. Write Goddess Laxmi's mantra **SHREEM** too.
4. In the square part of the grid, write the amount required in the middle. Place your picture over it or write the name of your business on a chit and place over the written amount. You can put both as well. Place your choice of stone over it and say thrice: *Be my lucky charm to bring in new financial opportunities and extra income.*
5. Place Green Aventurine on the bottom 2 points of the square and say thrice: *Bring in new financial opportunities.*
6. Place Citrine on each top point of the square (bottom points of the triangle) and say thrice: *Increase in financial abundance.*
7. Place 1 Smoky Quartz at the top point of the triangle and between the 2 Green Aventurines on the bottom line (roof to ground connection). Say thrice: *To clear blockages and create a clear pathway.*
8. Trace the house with the wand connecting all of the stones. Say thrice: *Money flows to me, my house, my business and my family abundantly.*
9. Create a Chi Ball, put Reiki symbols (if you are attuned), pray to Goddess Fortuna, Goddess Laxmi and Archangel Ariel: *Please shower gold coins in the form of money of any currency to help me, my family and house prosper with financial abundance.* Release on grid.

Keep this active until your wish manifests.

Bring Best Partner Crystal Grid

This crystal grid is meant for singles to attract their best life partner. The magic of crystals and Divine energies of Reiki along with the geometric pattern of the grid bring a miraculous outcome. The grid base is a Star of David. It has 2 triangles intersecting with each other.

Required

Rose Quartz- 2
Carnelian- 2
Green Aventurine- 2
Clear Quartz cluster/geode/rock
Selenite Wand

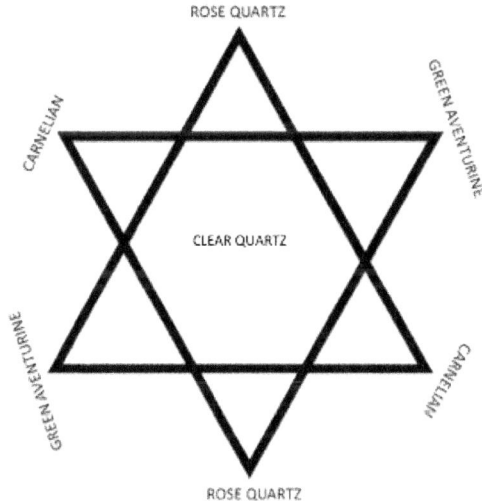

1. On the top point, place Rose Quartz. As you place Rose Quartz, say thrice: *Bring the right person I deserve.*
2. On the left bottom point and top right point, place Green Aventurine. As you place it, say thrice: *Bring opportunities to attract the best partner.*

3. On the last 2 points, place Carnelian and say thrice: *To intensify search and focus on bringing the right partner.*
4. Place your picture or name written on paper at the centre and place Clear Quartz over it, say thrice: *Amplify the energy of the grid.*
5. With a wand, trace the Star of David over the grid, connecting all the stones point to point.
6. Make a Chi Ball, put Reiki symbols and any other symbols you wish into the Chi Ball. While making it pray to Archangel Chamuel: *Dear Archangel Chamuel, please make my right partner's soul hear my call and bring him/her to me. Thank you.*
7. Visualize your desired outcome. Release the Chi Ball on the grid. Leave it for a minimum of 21 days.

Hope all the singles manifest their right partner very soon.

Angelic Grid to Charge Crystals

As you work with crystals more and more, you will realize you need to charge crystals with Divine energies after cleansing and before programming. There are multiple ways to charge crystals and setting an Angel grid to charge crystals works best when you have multiple crystals to charge.

Here we will magnify the energies by using Angelic Zibu symbols. The Zibu symbols used are Universal Love, Divine Essence, Blessings, Unlimited Abundance, and Effortless Connection. These symbols don't require any attunement.

Other symbols used are Aum and Cho Ku Rei. Aum needs no attunement so anyone can use it. It is the ultimate powerful symbol and considered to be the symbol of Divine Creation.

Cho Ku Rei needs attunement so only Reiki 2nd degree channels can use this. If you are not attuned to Reiki then skip drawing it, don't use. Continue without Cho Ku Rei.

The base used for the grid is a pentagram because it is one of the most powerful symbols of protection. When we charge our crystals, we want our grids to be protected from unwanted energies.

Required

Crystal angel statues any size, any stone- 5
Clear Quartz or Amethyst pencils- 5
Wand

1. On paper, draw a pentagram or take a print-out of a pentagram. Draw Cho Ku Rei on 4 corners of the paper to seal the energies. Draw Angelic Zibu Symbols as shown in the grid diagram.
2. Draw AUM at the centre.
3. Place each angel statue on 5 points of the star just below angels.
4. Place pencils inside the triangles of the star. Pencils are used to direct energies towards the centre. So, angelic energies from statues are directed towards the centre stones via pencils.
5. Place crystals to be cleansed at the centre on top of the symbol AUM. You can place directly on the symbol; you can put the bowl of crystals or you can even place a jar of crystals at the centre.
6. Now that your grid is set, take your wand and make a clockwise circle over the grid thrice, saying: *I charge this grid to infuse all the crystals on AUM / in bowl / in jar with angelic Divine energies.*

You can pick up your stones after a minimum of 4-5 hours. You can keep the grid and keep replacing centre stones to be charged.

This is one of the most powerful ways to infuse your stones with angelic energies.

Violet Flame Transmutation with Amethyst Grid

Violet Flame transmutes all negative energies to positive, transmutes negative karmas to light and releases all blockages. In this grid, we will be using only Amethyst as Amethyst is the stone associated with Archangel Zadkiel and he is one of the keepers of the Violet Flame. This grid brings about deep transformation within us.

Required

Amethyst cluster/ big crystal
Minimum 8 Amethyst tumbled stones

1. First, cleanse all stones. Program all tumbled stones to transmute all negative to positive with Violet Flame energies.

2. Take the Amethyst cluster or a big crystal and draw Hon Sha Ze Sho Nen over it, and connect it with the energies of Archangel Zadkiel and St. Germain.

3. Take a printout of the Flower of Life layout and colour it in various shades of purple.

4. Place your Amethyst cluster/ crystal at the centre of the grid. Place tumbled stones on the grid wherever you feel guided. You can use as many tumbled stones as you are guided to use though the minimum should be 8. Don't copy any layout online, just follow your own intuition.

> As you place 1st stone, say: *I am a being of Violet fire, I am the purity God desires.*
>
> As you place 2nd stone, say: *Clear negative energy residues from across lives from my mind, body, soul and aura.*
>
> As you place 3rd stone, say: *Release what doesn't serve me anymore.* (You can add family members' names as well)
>
> As you place 4th stone, say: *Transmute all negative energy surrounding me to positive on a daily basis.*
>
> Repeat from 1 as you add more stones.

5. Take Amethyst, Clear Quartz or Selenite wand and rotate over the grid thrice clockwise and say: *I now release and transmute all negative energies and welcome new growth and new positive energies. I now call the Violet Flame of transmutation, Archangel Zadkiel and St. Germain to burn away all that doesn't serve me and my family, hinders our progress and drains our energies. Thank You.*

You can set this grid in your house or workplace. So many people come and leave residues of their energies, so this grid will also help clear negative energies on a daily basis. Keep this grid for a minimum of 21 days. You can reset it again and again.

Crystals for Weight Loss

Are you one of those people who want to lose weight but you are big foodie and have no time to exercise? Or are you one of those who hardly eats anything but still gains weight? Are you someone who has a poor metabolism? Haven't we all tried diet plans, slimming pills, detoxification programs and what not? Let us make weight loss a little easier with Crystals and Reiki.

I am listing a few crystals that will help with weight loss. The first and foremost thing to do is cleanse your crystal. Draw Cho Ku Rei on the crystal and rotate coned fingers 7 times over it anti-clockwise saying. *Cleanse*. Next draw Cho Ku Rei again over your crystal and rotate coned fingers 7 times over it clockwise saying: *Purify*. Now draw other symbols that you are attuned to over the crystal (let your intuition guide you as to which symbols to draw). Program your crystal for weight loss and give Reiki for about 5 minutes.

Below are Some Crystals which Help with Weight Loss.

Amethyst- Reduces cravings. Extremely helpful when you are trying to control your appetite. Great for addictive eating disorder.

Blue Apatite- The healing properties of this stone contradict its name. Apatite suppresses your appetite so it is a great stone to work with when you are preparing for a weight loss plan.

Bloodstone- Stimulates detoxification, helps elevate metabolism.

Carnelian- When you want to munch in-between meals, make sure you have Carnelian in your palms. It helps detoxify the body and improve general health.

Citrine- Eliminates what you do not need- physically or emotionally. Improves digestion.

Clear Topaz- Improves metabolism to burn more calories.

Goldstone- Helps you to hold on to your diet goals.

Iolite- Helps detoxify the liver and release fats deposited throughout the body (especially love-handles).

Kyanite- Wear it around the Throat chakra to boost your immune system. It increases willpower, hence it assists in resisting snacking and munching. Also used for people who are chronically overweight.

Rose Quartz- Brings self-love. It helps with emotional detoxification and so reduces eating disorders.

Seraphinite- Creates detoxification process in the body which helps with losing weight.

Sodalite- Helps to reach balance and boost metabolism.

Sunstone- Suppresses hunger and improves metabolism.

Tiger's Eye- Improves digestion and speeds up metabolism.

Yellow Apatite- The vibrations of Yellow Apatite help to remove stagnant energies from the Solar Plexus chakra when placed over the chakra. It removes anger that is deep-rooted in the cells and tissues.

- **Supreme combo for weight loss - Apatite, Seraphinite and Sunstone.**
- **Weight Loss on a physical, mental and emotional level - Apatite, Amethyst and Carnelian.**

The above stones have more healing properties but I have only pointed out how they help with weight loss.

How to use these stones for weight loss:

- Make crystal water with a single stone or combination.
- Carry it with you in a pocket, purse or bag.
- Wear it as a pendant, necklace or bracelet.
- Put it under your pillow.
- Meditate with the stone.
- Make a crystal grid for weight loss.
- Keep a bowl of crystals beside your fridge.
- While eating, hold your crystal in your palm and state that your body will only accept what is needed at this time and discharge anything that is not needed.

This combination of Crystals and Reiki, along with nutritional diet and exercise, manifests weight loss much quicker.

Crystals for Money

Why do we need money? Is our necessity for money only limited to basic needs? The need for money depends on the lifestyle you want to live. You need money to fulfil your dreams and achieve your goals.

Crystals have energies and powers that originate from Earth. By working with 'Money Stones', you can accelerate manifesting abundance and prosperity. Let us make manifesting money a little easier with Crystals and Reiki.

I am listing few special crystals that will boost your ability to make money flow in your direction. The first and foremost thing to do is cleanse your crystal. Draw Cho Ku Rei on the crystal and rotate coned fingers 7 times over it anti-clockwise saying: **Cleanse**. Next draw Cho Ku Rei again over your crystal and rotate coned fingers 7 times over it clockwise saying: **Purify**. Now draw other symbols that you are attuned to over the crystal (let your intuition guide you as to which symbols to draw). Program your crystal with money affirmations and give Reiki for about 5 minutes.

Crystals for Money:

- **Citrine** - Citrine is known as the ***Merchant's Stone***. It is one of the abundance stones that generate amazing and mystical qualities to attract wealth and to amplify manifestation power.
- **Green Aventurine** - This crystal is best described as a stone of luck or chance. It is also referred as a Money Stone. It brings fortune, money, luck, and provides more chances to increase your wealth.
- **Peridot** - It clears blockages related to manifestations. This crystal is best if you are struggling with debt. It has the power to increase your wealth as well as health.
- **Malachite** - This crystal attracts the right people that can help you achieve more wealth and prosperity (attracts clients, improves business). It also has a tendency to protect your money.
- **Pyrite** - It is known as ***Fool's Gold***. It will help you invest money carefully and wisely, ensuring no one can fool you. It blocks all negativity and speeds up manifestation.
- **Jade** - Place Jade near your wallet and money jar to attract more wealth and abundance easily.
- **Clear Quartz/Smoky Quartz** - These are both multi-purpose stones and are considered all-rounders. Place these crystals on a few notes of currency and leave it outside in the sunlight for a few hours with the intention to bring more money.
- **Ruby** - It is known as the ***Gambler's Stone***. When you are gambling, make sure to wear or carry Ruby. Keep wearing this crystal and you may even end up marrying a millionaire.
- **Sunstone** - It releases and brings positive energy even during your worst financial phase.
- **Tiger's Eye** - It can even change disastrous financial situations to your benefit by giving calm and logical insights.
- **Moon Stone** - In many parts of the world, people consider the moon a money magnet. Moon Stone has the energy of the moon and the moon is known to be associated with money.

The above stones have more healing properties but I have only pointed out how they help with money and abundance.

How to use these crystals for money:

- Make crystal water with a single stone or combination.
- Carry it with you in a pocket, purse or bag.
- Wear it as a pendant, necklace or bracelet.
- Put it under your pillow.
- Write your abundance wish on paper with Reiki symbols drawn on it and place it under the crystal.
- Write your wish on paper invoking symbols and wrap it around your crystal.
- Meditate with the stone.
- Make a crystal grid for wealth and prosperity.

Welcome the wealth into your life!

Crystals for Love and Relationships

Love is in the air. We all want pure, unconditional and everlasting love. So let us again combine two powerful modalities, Crystals and Reiki, to attract new love or repair strained relationships. Listed are a few top crystals which harmonize relationships and help bring true love.

The first and foremost thing to do is cleanse your crystal. Draw Cho Ku Rei on your crystal and rotate coned fingers 7 times over it anti-clockwise saying: **Cleanse**. Next draw Cho Ku Rei again over your crystal and rotate coned fingers 7 times over it clockwise saying: **Purify**. Now draw other symbols that you are attuned to over the crystal (let your intuition guide you as to which symbols to draw). Program your crystal with love, relationship and harmony affirmations and give Reiki for about 5 minutes.

Rose Quartz - Rose Quartz tops the chart when it comes to *love and relationships*. It is the crystal for unconditional and pure love. It wards off negativity, anger and resentment and replaces it with love. It also mends broken hearts as well as healing current relationships.

Morganite - It is pink in colour and known as the cousin of Aquamarine and Emerald. It connects with unconditional universal love and aligns the heart with its Divine plan. It attracts abundance of love, increases ability to accept love, heals broken hearts and restores difficult relationships. Morganite is also known as the *Angel's Stone* as it makes communications with angels easier.

Red Tourmaline/Ruby - Red Tourmaline is also known as Rubellite because of its close resemblance to Ruby. Red Tourmaline and Ruby both work best to heal emotional wounds. They bring Universal Love and help heal depression.

Emerald - Emeralds radiate the purest form of green rays. Green is the colour of the Heart chakra; emerald brings balance to the Heart chakra. Emerald is known as *The stone of successful love*. It is said that gifting Emerald to your loved ones brings them closer to you as it vibrates and radiates love.

Rhodochrosite - It is a great stone to collaborate with the Heart chakra. It helps those who are dealing with emotional loss. It brings comfort, positivity and promotes self-love. It also acts as a bridge between two people who have drifted apart. If you wish to reconnect with someone, place Rhodochrosite on their picture, say their name thrice while holding the stone and ask them to connect to you.

Malachite - It clears blockages related to love and the heart. It helps to heal heartache and bring new true love. It can also bring harmony to all kinds of relationships. (Note: ***Do not put Malachite in mouth or make elixir of it***)

Dioptase - It awakens the Heart chakra promoting love, harmony and compassion, and heals emotional pain. It helps release negative emotions related to a broken heart, divorce or death. It also breaks karmic patterns by working with past life issues.

Orange and Red Carnelian - It helps rekindle passion in strained and difficult relationships. It helps those going through a mid-life crisis, especially males. It also reduces possessiveness and jealousy in relationships.

Green Aventurine - It protects and clears blockages from the Heart chakra, bringing the ability to attract true love and maintain harmonious relationships.

Watermelon Tourmaline - It helps to remove guilt and enhances the ability to move on and bring true love.

Peridot - It releases old negative patterns and vibrations, creating space for Universal Love.

The above stones have more healing properties but I have only pointed out how they help with love and relationships.

How to use crystals for love and relationships:

- Make crystal water with a single stone or combination (Note**:** Do **not** put Malachite in mouth or make elixir of it).
- Carry it with you in a pocket, purse or bag.
- Wear it as a pendant, necklace or bracelet.
- Put it under your pillow.
- Write your wish on paper invoking symbols and wrap it around your crystal.
- Meditate with the stone.
- Make a crystal grid for love and harmonious relationships.
- Place by your bedside or relationship corner.

Crystals for Healing Pets

Crystal healing and Reiki combined bring remarkable results for humans as well as for animals. Animals have an amazing ability to sense the properties of crystals. They are very receptive and adaptive towards crystals and hence it is a good idea to heal them with crystals and Reiki. Pets are our babies; we love them and nurture them like our own children. So why not heal them and protect them with Reiki and crystals? My dog Pari wears a Clear Quartz pendant, which I cleanse, charge and program with Reiki for her highest good.

The first and foremost thing to do is cleanse your crystal. Draw Cho Ku Rei on the crystal and rotate coned fingers 7 times over it anti-clockwise saying: **Cleanse**. Next draw Cho Ku Rei again over your crystal and rotate coned fingers 7 times over it clockwise saying: **Purify**. Now draw other symbols that you are attuned to over the crystal (let your intuition guide you as to which symbols to draw). Program your crystal for your pet's highest good (or particular issue) and give Reiki for about 5 minutes.

Below is the list of problems and crystals for healing

Agate - Calms and relaxes your pet, balances energy and chakras.
Amber - Flea and ticks.
Amethyst - Master healer, pain, excessive barking, can be used for everything.
Bloodstone - Calms anxiousness, promotes sleep.
Blue Fluorite - Allergies, bones and respiratory system.
Carnelian - Aging pets, allergies, arthritis, cancer, skin issues.
Clear Quartz - Master Healer, can be used for everything.
Citrine - Diabetes, hyperactivity, intestine issues, stress, training.
Coral - Bladder, emotional stability, kidney.
Garnet - Reproductive organs.
Green Fluorite - Blood purification, lymph and respiratory systems.
Hematite - Grounding, muscular problems.
Jade – Abused pets, aggression, calms, helps eye issues.
Jasper - Digestion. Adding a few drops of Jasper elixir to food will help with pet's digestion.
Kyanite - Aligns all chakras.
Labradorite - Aura protection.
Lapis Lazuli - Pain, respiratory issues.
Moonstone - Bonding, calming, cancer, digestion.
Rose Quartz - Abused pets, aggression, reduces fear and stress, wounds.
Smoky Quartz - Nervous system issues.
Sodalite - Calms your pet, reduces stress, training.
Tiger's eye - Grounding, protection, travel.

How to use crystals with pets:

- Place crystals somewhere near your pet's auric field. Make sure to put it out of reach.
- Attach the crystal pendant to their collar.
- Spray crystal water/elixir on pet.
- Massage with crystal wand if your pet permits.
- Place ethereal crystal directly over the problematic area.

- Write a note invoking symbols for pet's wellbeing and wrap it around the crystal or just put it under the crystal.

Do not forget to cleanse and charge your crystals with Reiki to remove accumulated unwanted/negative energies.

The Full Body Crystal Layout

The full body crystal layout is based on emotional healing that heals the root cause of issues. It focuses on grounding, stability, strength, regeneration, focus, immunity, expansion, accomplishment, restructure, joy, release, voice, emotions, tranquillity, self-love and spirit. This will cleanse and activate your full-body system.

Below is the list of crystals, their purpose and where to place on the body. Each stone should be cleansed and charged. This layout works best with in-person healing.

Stone	Purpose	Body Area
Hematite x2	Grounding	Feet
Tiger's Eye x2	Stability	Knees
Garnet x2	Strength	Thighs
Red Tiger's Eye x2	Regenerate cells	Hips
Red Jasper x1	Root Chakra point	Root Chakra

Carnelian x1	Focus	Lower Abdomen (Sacral)
Peach Moonstone x2	Immunity	Kidney, Spleen
Citrine x1	Expansion	Solar Plexus
Jade x1	Accomplishment	Liver
Moss Agate x2	Restructure	Lungs
Green Aventurine x1	Heart Centre point	Heart Chakra
Rose Quartz x1	Emotional Release	Higher Heart Chakra
Amazonite x2	Release	Shoulder
Black Tourmaline x1	Balance	Palm (right)
Clear Quartz x1	Balance	Palm (left)
Lapis Lazuli x1	Joy	Throat (Throat chakra)
Sodalite x1	Voice	Mouth/jaw
Blue Kyanite x1	Trust	Third Eye Chakra
Amethyst x6	Emotions	Eyes/Ears/Nose
Clear Quartz x1	Tranquillity	Crown Chakra
Selenite x1	Spirit	Over head
Smoky Quartz x depends on your height. Approximate.	Rest	Body outline at intervals

Notes

1. Smoky Quartz is placed at regular gaps a little away from the body, not touching the body, like forming a body shape. You can replace the above stones with any stone that is related to that chakra.

2. Nose- Put 2 Amethysts beside nostrils.
3. Start from feet to crown or crown to feet.

Once the stones are placed, lie down and relax for 20 minutes. You can give Reiki to each area where the stones are placed to amplify the energies. You can put multiple stones on each organ if you wish.

After 20 minutes, remove stones one by one. Drop these stones in salt water as you remove, as it absorbs negative energies.

Crystal Water for Healing

All crystals and gemstones have different properties and unique abilities to heal. I am not writing about crystal healing and laying of stones. I am writing about Healing with Crystal Water/Essence. A few days back, during the wee hours, I was in a deep sleep and out of nowhere I heard **Crystal Water** in my mind. I was confused as to where this thought popped up from. I took it as a sign from angels.

So later during the day, I started looking up on the Internet about it. And Bingo! I found lots of many wonderful techniques for healing.

I tried the simplest one to make crystal water. So far I have made Rose Quartz water, Citrine water and Clear Quartz water. Crystal essence or crystal water has been used for healing purposes for countless years. It can be made easily and can be stored to re-use. There are many ways to make crystal water. Some add vodka or vinegar as preservatives. I prefer making it simpler way as I do not like preservatives. Crystal water made without preservatives may last up to 20 days. Make sure that you do not use just any crystal as some crystals may have toxic components. *Study crystal properties before using them.*

Here are two ways to make Crystal Water:

- Choose the crystal or crystals per your issue. If you want to make money essence use Citrine or if you want love you can use Rose Quartz.
- Ground yourself. Stay calm and relaxed. Pray or meditate.
- Cleanse your crystal. Hold it in your palm. Invoke an angel's help, ask your crystals for help. Draw Reiki symbols and infuse the flow of Reiki. State your intention and give Reiki to your crystal for about 5-10 minutes. Hold your intention while charging your crystal with Reiki. To heal others, dedicate the symbol to someone by stating their name 3 times along with the intention.

Now here we have the 2 ways to make crystal water:

- Take 2 glass containers, one big and one small. Put your Reiki-infused crystal in the small container and if possible close the container. Fill the big container with spring water or filtered water. Place the small container with the crystal in the big container. Take care that the container with the crystal doesn't topple. Put the containers out in sunlight or moonlight for 4-5 hours. Your crystal water is ready.
- Another method is simpler. Put your Reiki-infused crystal directly in a glass container filled with spring water or filtered water. Leave your container in sunlight or moonlight for few hours. Your crystal water is ready.
- When your crystal water is half consumed, you can add more water to it and again leave it in sunlight or moon light.
- Additionally, you can place extra crystals pointed towards the container around the container.
- Alternatively, you can let crystals sit in water for 24 hours and then use it.
- Once every 15-20 days cleanse your container, crystals and do the above process to refill and recharge.

- Pour this water into a dark coloured bottle like cobalt blue or green.
- The more crystals you put in, the stronger the crystal water is.
- Mix 5-6 drops of crystal water with drinking water to consume.
- When consuming this water, make sure that crystals stay in the container and don't drop in your glass.
- You can carry this water to school, your office or wherever you go, to keep you charged with crystal healing.
- You can water your plants with crystal water, with 3-4 drops of crystal water added to 1 glass of water.
- It is safe for pets too. Add 3-4 drops of crystal water to 1 bowl of water.
- Fill a spray bottle and spray on yourself or the affected person.
- Remove negativity from your home or workspace by spraying crystal water.
- Can be applied directly to skin.
- Crystal Water is also known as: crystal elixirs, gem elixirs, gem waters, crystal tonics, gem tonics, gem essences, crystal essence and more.
- If you decide to use more than one type of crystal, make sure the properties of the crystals are compatible. Try not make 'crystal chaos' by adding too many.
- Double-check crystals' properties before putting in water as some are **HIGHLY TOXIC**. For 'risky' stones always use Method 1.

Be innovative and make use of crystal water as much as you can!

Prosperity Spray

Money is an essential part of our life- to achieve desired goals and fulfil our own and our family's dreams. Along with hard work to achieve goals, adding a little magic won't harm, wouldn't you say?

You will need lots of stuff to make a powerful prosperity spray.

- Green/Golden candle
- Archangel Ariel/Goddess Laxmi/Goddess Abundantia/Goddess Fortuna picture or statue
- Tarot - Empress, 9 of Pentacles and 9 of Cups
- Crystals - Citrine, Jade, Tiger's Eye, Green Aventurine and any other money stones you have
- Essential Oil - Blend of 3 drops gardenia essential oil + 3 drops peppermint oil + 3 drops cinnamon oil + 2 drops bay oil (you can also add basil oil, ginger oil or patchouli oil)
- Herbs - Basil, a cinnamon stick, 4 cloves, 1 dried ginger root and 1 star anise
- Cup of rock salt or Himalayan salt
- 1 litre water in a bowl
- Spray bottle

1. On your candle, carve 'Wealth'. On the other side of the candle, draw Reiki symbols. Anoint with the prosperity oil you blended. Light it and place it in front of picture/statue of Goddess/ Angel.
2. Take a cleansed stone. Program it to attract more money into your life. Give Reiki to it or charge with mantra or prayers. Place the stones beside the candle.
3. Place oil blends and herbs beside the candle.
4. Make a circle in front of the candle the size of the bowl with salt. Draw Cho Ku Rei with finger inside the circle. Place all 3 tarot cards piled up on each other. Place your water bowl on the cards.
5. Add crystals, herbs and 8-10 drops of your oil blend to the water. Stir thrice with the cinnamon stick and put it in the water as well.
6. Touch your water bowl with both hands and pray: *Dear God, Goddess Laxmi, Lord Narayana, Archangel Ariel, Goddess Abundantia, Fortuna and Tara and Universal Life Force Energy (Reiki), please channel your power and energies into this water to bless me, my family, my home, my work, my bank accounts and money box with financial prosperity. Infuse this water with magical power of financial abundance and prosperity to bestow on me, my family, my home, my work, my bank accounts and money box. Thank you, Thank you, Thank you.*
7. Leave the bowl on the altar till the candle burns out. Later sieve the water and decant into a clean spray bottle. Spray on self, family, home, office, and money box, and put a drop on cheque book or pass book.

This seems like a lot of work and ingredients but it is very powerful too.

Psychic Attacks and Crystals

Psychic attacks occur when negative and evil energies are directed towards you with deliberate or undeliberate intentions. It is extremely important to protect ourselves and our loved ones from psychic attacks, psychic vampires and all sort of evil eyes.

What are the symptoms of being psychically attacked?

- Irritation all the time
- Frequent mood swings
- Anger for no reason
- Sudden fatigue
- Sudden nightmares
- Lack of focus and concentration
- Easily influenced by others
- Feeling threatened
- Staying fearful
- Falling sick frequently

- Less immunity than before
- Sudden change in character
- Lack of clarity in thinking
- Sudden energy loss
- Sudden depression
- Hallucination
- Obsessive negative thoughts
- Hearing weird voices
- Ongoing bad luck
- Crying for no reason
- Paranoia
- Sudden goose-bumps for no reason
- Restlessness
- Bruises on body parts after sleeping
- And more…..

I will list a few common crystals that protect your physical as well as auric body from psychic attacks. These stones have other healing properties too of course.

Amethyst - Amethyst is an all-purpose stone. As a protection stone, it protects against witchcraft, dark energies, black magic and evil eyes. It is also considered one of the best stones to carry during travel.

Bloodstone - Protects against entities and all forms of harmful spirits and provides total psychic protection.

Black Tourmaline - Very powerful stone against psychic attacks and wards off dark and negative energies. It is one of the stones that can also transmute negative energies to light.

Black Obsidian/ Black Onyx - Psychic defence, blocks negative influences.

Carnelian - Protects from injuries, wards off harmful spirits, and blocks others' attempts to read your thoughts.

Jasper - Returns negative energy back to its origin.

Tiger's Eye - Protects against unwanted energy forms (negative thoughts and spirits).

Clear Quartz - Transmutes negative to positive.

Black Kyanite - Destroys negativity and attacks coming towards you.

Lapis Lazuli - Creates a protective shield, returns psychic attacks to sender.

Fluorite - Acts as a guard against psychic attacks.

Peridot - Powerful shield against dark energies and all kinds of psychic forces.

Grey Jasper - Powerful protection stone in general, strong protection against black magic.

Mica - Protects against anger and eliminates negative personality traits.

These are just a few common crystals listed above. There are of course many more crystals that work against psychic attacks.

How to Use

- Make crystal water with a single stone or combination (Note: Check crystals' properties before putting in water. Some crystals are toxic.)
- Spray crystal water on your aura.
- Carry it with you in a pocket, purse or bag.
- Wear it as a pendant, necklace or bracelet.
- Put it under your pillow.
- Write your wish on paper invoking symbols and wrap it around your crystal.
- Meditate with the stone.
- Make a crystal grid for protection.
- Place anywhere in the house or workplace.

Stay safe and protected!

Diverting Psychic Attacks

Psychic attacks are basically negative energies or negative intentions directed towards us knowingly or unknowingly. We try to perform grounding, protecting and shielding daily but the fact is there are days when, due to lack of time or whatever reason, we fail to do grounding and shielding. To avoid any such scenario, wouldn't you love it if there were something that absorbs all negativity directed towards you? Yes, we can program our crystals to divert all negativity coming towards us to itself. The crystal will absorb all negativity and bad intentions directed towards you without letting it reach you.

Technique to Divert All the Negative Energy to a Crystal

1. After cleansing the crystal, hold it in your dominant hand. Draw Reiki symbols and enable the Reiki flow, fill the crystal with Reiki energy. It may take about 3-5 minutes.

2. Now bring your crystal to your Third Eye and direct a white light from the Third Eye into the crystal. To program your crystal, say: *From this very moment on, absorb all negativity directed*

towards me intentionally or unintentionally. Absorb all negativity before it comes in contact with me. Transmute all absorbed negativity to light.

3. Carry this crystal with you if you are going out. Keep in a room where you feel there is lots of negativity oozing. Program the crystal for shops and offices as there are umpteen numbers of people around. For shops and offices, program the crystal to absorb all negativity projected towards you and your office or shop.

4. Cleanse the crystal frequently to clear away accumulated negative energy and reprogram again for further use.

A few common Protection Crystals are:

- **Protection from evil and evil eye** - Eye Agate, Carnelian, Topaz, Cat's Eye, Pyrite, Black Tourmaline, Malachite, Turquoise and more…

- **Protection from negativity** - Black Tourmaline, Black Onyx, Black Obsidian, Citrine, Smoky Quartz, Clear Quartz and more…

- **Protection for children** - Black Tourmaline, Blue Agate, Malachite, Jade, Ruby and more…

- **Protection during pregnancy** - Black Tourmaline, Moonstone, Malachite, Jasper, Ammonite, Rose Quartz and more…

- **Physical protection** - Carnelian, Fluorite, Zircon, Black Tourmaline, Agate, Smoky Quartz and more…

So, divert all the psychic attacks coming towards you using any of the above crystals and stay healthy, wealthy, safe and happy.

Psychic Surgery with Crystal Wands

Psychic Surgery is a virtual method of surgery to remove old debris, blockages, negativities, thought-forms, and memory imprints from your auric field and body. It is a powerful yet gentle method of treatment. It removes the root cause of the problem which, if not dealt with, can cause anguish and suffering.

This article is about doing psychic surgery with crystal wands. You require one Selenite wand and the other one can be any wand, whatever you have.

1. Cleanse your wands and charge with Reiki energy.
2. Protect yourself by drawing Cho Ku Rei on your 7 chakras and on your palms.
3. Imagine yourself as a doctor and Selenite wand as your scalpel.
4. Draw a big Cho Ku Rei on the area where psychic surgery is to be performed. Now with your Selenite wand make an imaginary incision on the area in the air.
5. With your Selenite wand, dig and scrape out all the debris and blockages (the same way you scrape rust or dirt from an object).
6. Now point your Selenite wand towards the scrapped debris and blockages and imagine all the debris,

blockages, negativities, thought-forms and memory imprints been suctioned by the wand. Keep rotating your wand and imagine the area is totally cleansed.
7. Keep your Selenite wand aside. Now take your other wand and point it towards the cleansed area. Draw Cho Ku Rei and Dai Ko Myo in the air with this wand. Imagine Cho Ku Rei and Dai Ko Myo multiplying and filling the whole cleansed area.
8. Call upon Archangel Raphael and ask him to fill the area with Divine emerald green light. Point your wand towards the area and imagine the whole area is filled with green healing light.
9. Once you feel it is done, draw a big Cho Ku Rei and say: *Seal, Seal, Seal.*
10. Thank Archangel Raphael and Reiki.

Here the Selenite wand is used to remove all the negative energies while the other wand is used to fill the area with light.

Cleansing with a Pendulum

I think the pendulum is one of the most underrated tools for healing. It can do way more than give yes or no answers to your queries. And when it is merged with Reiki energy, the result is profound. I personally don't use a pendulum for yes/no, but my pendulum is my saviour when it comes to cleansing. Cleansing chakras, aura or space, I use a pendulum for all.

Chakra Cleansing I

1. Cleanse your pendulum and draw the Reiki symbols over it. Give Reiki to it for 5 minutes with the intention to cleanse, unblock and balance all the chakras.
2. Ask your client to lie down and draw Cho Ku Rei on each chakra. Now hover the pendulum over the Root chakra and ask it to cleanse and unblock the chakra. Let the pendulum swing (swinging direction varies from pendulum to pendulum). Once it stops, ask the pendulum to balance the chakra and fill it with Divine light. Let it swing till it stops. Do the same method for all the chakras.

You can also place chakra stones over the chakras and then continue with the above method.

Chakra Cleansing II

This is another method of chakra cleansing in which you don't need your client in-person or a substitute dummy.

1. Draw a distant symbol over the pendulum and intone Hon Sha Ze Sho Nen thrice. Say thrice: *Connect to xyz (client's name)*. Again, draw a distant symbol intoning the name thrice, and say thrice: *Connect to xyz's Root chakra.*
3. Hold your pendulum over empty space and ask it to cleanse Root chakra and let it swing. Once it stops, ask the pendulum to balance the chakra and fill it with Divine light. Let it swing till it stops.
4. Again, draw distant symbol and connect to next chakra and do the above procedure. Do same for all the chakras.

Aura Cleansing

1. Take your cleansed pendulum and draw Reiki symbols over it. Give Reiki for 5 minutes with the intention to cleanse the aura.
2. Draw a distant symbol over the pendulum and connect it with the energies of your client.
3. Hold your pendulum over empty space and let it swing. It may take merely 2-3 minutes or may go on for about 15-20 minutes. Just sit patiently and let the pendulum do its work. Once it stops, ask the pendulum if the aura is cleansed. If it says no, continue doing the same next day as well.

Room Cleansing/ Space Clearing I

1. Sit in a room. Draw Reiki symbols and charge your pendulum with Reiki energy. Hold the pendulum and ask if the room has negative energies or entities. If it says yes, follow the given method below to cleanse the room. If it says no, go to another room and check.

2. Draw Reiki symbols that you are attuned to on the pendulum. Draw 3 Cho Ku Rei symbols. Give Reiki with the intention to cleanse the room from all sorts of negative energies and entities. Let it swing. Again, the time duration may vary from room to room. Have patience and let the pendulum do all the cleansing.
3. Once it is done, ask the pendulum if the room has negative energies or entities. If it says yes, do the above method again. If it says no, go to the next room and carry on with the above method.

Room Cleansing/ Space Clearing II

If you are doing distant cleansing, draw Hon Sha Ze Sho Nen over the pendulum and connect it to each of the client's rooms, one by one. Hold the pendulum and let it swing till it stops. The method is same as above, except here you connect the pendulum to your client's rooms.

Crystals and Chakras

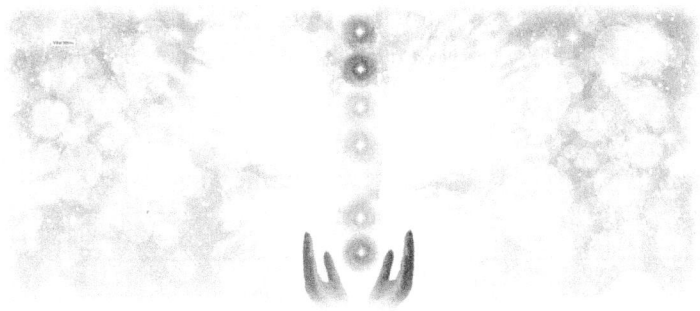

Crystals have been used for healing since ancient times. Each crystal has its own multiple healing properties, which help harmonize mind, body and soul.

I am a crystal-obsessed person, I simply love being around crystals. Crystals can be used for chakra healing; simply pick a crystal that resonates with the affected chakra, cleanse it, program and charge it with Reiki and it is ready for use. It is so simple.

Now many people face the question, which crystal to pick for which chakra. Listed below are some crystals that can be used for particular chakras.

Chakras	Crystals
Earth Star	Black Kyanite, Black Tourmaline, Black Obsidian, Dalmatian Jasper, Red Jasper, Granite, Smoky Quartz
Root Chakra	Red Jasper, Granite, Bloodstone, Hematite, Smoky Quartz, Black Tourmaline, Black Obsidian, Grey Jasper,

	Red Tiger's Eye, Snowflake Obsidian
Sacral Chakra	Carnelian, Orange Calcite, Orange Kyanite, Moonstone, Fluorite, Sunstone
Solar Plexus Chakra	Tiger's Eye, Citrine, Gold Quartz, Yellow Aventurine, Pyrite, Amber, Camel Agate
Heart Chakra	Rose Quartz, Pink Tourmaline, Green Aventurine, Emerald, Malachite, Jade, Peridot
Higher Heart	Aqua Amazonite, Green Tourmaline, Malachite, Rose Quartz, Pink Tourmaline, Emerald
Throat Chakra	Blue Kyanite, Turquoise, Lapis Lazuli, Blue Lace Agate, Sodalite, Amazonite
Third Eye Chakra	Amethyst, Kyanite, Iolite, Selenite, Lapis Lazuli, Sapphire, Sodalite, Rainbow Moonstone, Sugilite
Crown Chakra	Amethyst, Howlite, Clear Quartz, Selenite, White Calcite, Sugilite
Soul Star	Clear Quartz, Selenite, Angel Aura Quartz, Blue Kyanite, Labradorite

Use the above listed stones for chakra healing and issues related to particular chakras. Place the stones on a particular chakra and give Reiki, wear the stones, carry the programmed stones with you, keep in your house or workplace, keep at your altar… The list is endless.

Note - *The above listed crystals are just some of the many crystals that can be used for the particular chakras. Each stone can be used for multiple issues as per their properties. Example- Green Aventurine is a Heart chakra stone but it is also considered a money and luck stone; Tiger's Eye is considered a Solar Plexus stone but can also be used for money and protection.*

Aura Sweeping with Crystals

I would like to show you a way to heal your aura using crystals.

Select and cleanse your crystal. Draw Cho Ku Rei on the crystal and rotate coned fingers 7 times over it anti-clockwise saying: *Cleanse*. Next draw Cho Ku Rei again over your crystal and rotate coned fingers 7 times over it clockwise saying: *Purify*. Now draw other symbols that you are attuned to over the crystal (let your intuition guide you as to which symbols to draw). Program your crystal for aura healing and charge it for a minute with Reiki.

Now hold your crystal in your dominant hand. Rotate the crystal in large sweeping motions around your aura 7 times in a clockwise direction. Make sure you cover your aura from above your head to your toes. The best way to perform this method is to sit somewhere comfortably and continue.

The Best Crystals for Aura Healing Are:

Aura Cleanser - For general cleansing, use Lapis Lazuli or Black Tourmaline.
Aura Moods - To improve your aura mood, use Rutilated Quartz.
Aura Protection - Labradorite is the best stone for protecting your aura.
Aura Alignment - To align your aura layers, use Citrine.
Aura Booster - To energize your aura, use Sugilite.
Aura Holes - To heal your aura holes, use Amethyst.
Auric Tears - To heal auric tears, use Green Tourmaline.
Aura Repair - For general aura repair, use Carnelian.
Aura Negativity - To ward off negativity from aura, use Smoky Quartz.
Aura Strengthening - To strengthen the aura, use Magnetite.

These are just a few crystals mentioned above. You can also wear and carry these stones with you for aura protection. You can use crystal water/crystal elixirs too.

Distance Healing with Crystals

We are not unfamiliar with the amazing beauty and healing properties of crystals. Most of us are habituated with crystal grids for distant healing and manifestation. Not many are aware that even a single stone can be programmed for distant healing, though a crystal grid is more favourable as there are pencils placed that direct energy towards the main middle stone. Anyway, let me show you how to program a crystal to send distant healing without a grid.

Method 1

Pick a cleansed crystal that resonates with your issue. Hold it in your non-dominant palm and draw Hon Sha Ze Sho Nen, intoning its name thrice. Now connect the crystal to the person or the situation. Draw Cho Ku Rei and Sei He Ki and give Reiki to the crystal with your intention for about 10 minutes. Place the crystal somewhere safe or carry it with you always. Yes, it is that simple.

Suppose you want to manifest a wish, which doesn't include any person or situation- draw all the symbols on your stone and give Reiki visualizing or imagining your wish coming true.

Method 2

Pick a cleansed crystal. Bring it half an inch away from your Third Eye. Ask source energy to fill you with Divine white light. Beam white light into the crystal from your Third Eye. Draw symbols with this white light with your Third Eye on the crystal. State your intention and hold your thought for 68 seconds, visualizing the outcome. Place the crystal somewhere safe or carry it with you. *"Hold the thought for just 17 seconds and Law of Attraction kicks in. Hold a thought for 68 seconds and things move; manifestation has begun."* - Abraham Hicks

Method 3

Write your intention on a piece of paper, draw symbols and fold it. Place a cleansed and programmed crystal over it. That's it!

Try not to pick very tiny tumbled stones. You can use multiple stones for a single issue if they are tiny tumbled stones.

I have listed below some common issues and related crystals. These are by no means the only crystals related to the issues, there are many more. Also, crystals have multiple healing properties so each can be used for different issues too.

Stress/Worry - Amethyst, Clear Quartz, Garnet, Citrine, Smoky Quartz, Carnelian, Selenite.
Money/Career - Citrine, Green Aventurine, Tiger's Eye, Pyrite, Sunstone, Smoky Quartz, Jade, Moonstone, Carnelian.
Heart/Emotions - Rose Quartz, Green Aventurine, Moonstone, Ruby.
Weight loss - Tiger's Eye, Gold Quartz, Yellow Aventurine, Apatite, Bloodstone, Citrine, Kyanite, Amethyst.
Grounding - Red Jasper, Smoky Quartz, Camel Agate, Hematite, Kyanite, Black Tourmaline, Black Obsidian, Bloodstone,

Carnelian.

Protection - Black Tourmaline, Black Obsidian, Tiger's Eye, Grey Jasper, Mica Agate, Selenite, Kyanite.

Listed above are just basic issues and easily available crystals. Pick any as per your issue and program it for use.

20 Various Ways to Use Crystals

Once you have purchased your crystals, how do you start using your stones? What to do next once your crystals are home with you?

The first thing to do is cleanse, charge and program your crystals with intention. If you know Reiki, charge and program your stones with Reiki. Now that your crystals are cleansed, charged and programmed, what next? It depends on what you have purchased- jewellery, tumbled stones, clusters or any other form.

1. **Wear** - If your new crystal is in the form of jewellery, start wearing them. Wearing crystals is one of the best ways to use crystals as it is always near you and your aura.
2. **Under pillow** - Place the crystals under your pillow at night. You can place jewellery, tumbled stones, chips or any form that is safe to put under a pillow. Make sure it doesn't poke or

hurt you. If you are suffering from problems like insomnia and nightmares or you want psychic protection during sleep, then it is advisable to place your stones under your pillow.
3. **Crystal water (elixir)** - You can drink crystal water depending on the stones and the method used. You can spray crystal water on yourself, others, plants, pets or space, add it to bath water or you can use it during rituals. You can also add a few drops to shampoo, cream or any cosmetics you use. **If you are planning to drink elixir, make sure that your stones are non-toxic.**
4. **Decorative** - Put in your living room, bedroom or in fact any room as decorative pieces. You can place on a bedside table for better relationships, near the main door for protection, in your money box to attract more money and the living room for harmony. Place near electronic equipment to protect against EMF.
5. **Feng Shui** - Those who are into Feng Shui can place them as per Feng Shui Bagua.
6. **Bathing** – A few tumbled stones dropped in bathing bucket or bath tub.
7. **Body layout** - Place on each chakra for chakra healing or place on an affected organ.
8. **Massage** - Massage for beauty, to soothe pain and burns or to heal an affected area.
9. **Distant healing** - Program them for distant healing. If you know Reiki, you can use Hon Sha Ze Sho Nen to connect for distant healing.
10. **Meditation** - Hold your crystal in your palm and meditate. Clear Quartz or Angelite are among the best stones for meditation. You can meditate with crystals to make angelic connection easier.
11. **Intention slip** - Write your wish on paper. If you know Reiki, invoke Reiki symbols. Fold the slip and put it under the stone for a minimum of 21 days. Alternatively, take a few stones as per your issue and put them in a string bag along with your intention slip and carry with you or place on your altar.
12. **Decks and cards** - Putting Selenite or Black Tourmaline with decks keeps negative energies away. You can put Clear Quartz, Amethyst, Black Tourmaline, Labradorite, Selenite,

etc, while you do the reading for heightened intuition and psychic protection.
13. **Spells** - Use in any kind of spell, depending on the spell.
14. **Geodes** - Intention slips can be tucked inside a geode for fast manifestation. You can drink geode water by filling the geode with water and drinking after a few hours.
15. **Clusters** - Place your stones on self-cleansing crystal clusters for cleansing.
16. **Potting** - Place a few tumbled stones with plants for healthy growth.
17. **Cars** - Placing or hanging stones in cars or 2-wheelers protects against accidents, theft and robbery.
18. **Grids** - Make crystal grids for healing, manifesting, protection or any issues.
19. **Carry** - Carry stones with you in your pocket, hand bag, laptop bag or children's school bag as per issues.
20. Using as **bookmarks** helps to bring concentration and focus.

Be as creative as you want when using crystals.

About the Author

Rinku Patel is a Reiki Usui Master. She also practices Karmic Reiki, Kundalini Reiki, Angel Reiki, Crystal Healing, Dowsing, Soulmate Reiki, Angel Card, Tarot Card, Imara Reiki and Magnified Healing. Classes and Healing: Usui Reiki, Karmic Reiki, Kundalini Reiki, Angelic Reiki, Soulmate Reiki, Crystal Healing, Angel and Tarot Card Reading, Dowsing, Imara Reiki and Magnified Healing. Rinku can be reached via her email address, reikithemiraclehealing@gmail.com, and on Facebook at Reiki the Miracle Healing.